It is no exaggeration to say that I have ⟨preached?⟩ the whole of my Christian life! I have oft ⟨⟩ of the *Song of Solomon* but Malcolm M⟨aclean⟩ the rarefied heights and gives us new ⟨⟩ excellence of Christ. A fundamental desire which all believers have at the beginning of reading a book or listening to a sermon is, 'Sirs, we want to see Jesus.' This longing is more than answered by this book which appears to be the work of a Christ-obsessive. The sheer loveliness of Christ is found on virtually every line. Judicious cross-referencing to other portions of scripture as well as allusions to a robust theological framework convince us that *Royal Company* is far from fanciful in its interpretation. Maclean succeeds in showing that, 'Christ wishes to influence our emotions as well as inform our minds.' I cannot think of a healthier note to be sounded to contemporary evangelicalism.

The other strengths of *Royal Company* are that it steers a road between some of the sugar of past interpreters but avoids the spice of some contemporary 'expositors'. It also engages and graciously critiques the giants of the past like Durham, Burrows and Moody Stuart. It draws from the past and applies to the present. There is a paucity of decent expositions on the *Song* and it would not surprise me if this becomes a standard devotional work as well as a vital help to those of us who preach Christ glorious and crushed.

David Meredith,
Minister, Smithton Free Church of Scotland, Inverness, Scotland
and Chairman of Affinity

The poetry of the Song of Songs invites us into the greatest love story ever written. It is the love song of the King and his bride. Malcolm Maclean leads us in a sweet yet sober tour of this garden of divine love. He walks us through the Song devotionally, moving believers to long for deeper communion with the Son of God. Simultaneously, this book will encourage backsliders to run back into his loving arms.

Joel R. Beeke,
President, Puritan Reformed Theological Seminary,
Grand Rapids, Michigan

The Bible abounds in symbols, each of which – Shepherd, King, Lover, Husband, Lion, Lamb, etc., – exists to enhance our knowledge of God and our intimacy with him. Please let it come as no surprise to you that within the Bible there is one whole book in which symbols – and not only the marriage symbol – crowd together and cry out for interpretation. With Malcolm Maclean we are in safe hands. To be sure, his treatment of the Song extends interpretation into elaboration and application, and he will not carry every reader with him all the time, but everything he writes is true to the full biblical revelation of God in Christ, of the marvel of his love for us, and of our often faltering walk with him. Throughout he leaves us with strong aspirations to know Jesus better, to love him more deeply and steadily, and to grow in his truth and grace. And not aspirations only; his work helps us to achieve as well as aspire. He will put every reader deeply in his debt.

Alec Motyer,
Well-known expositor and commentary writer, Poynton, England

Deep in feeling and wide in application, this book shows a preacher's heart as well as a preacher's art. It makes no apology for opening up the Song as a commentary on the intimacy that ought to characterise our walk with the Lord Jesus Christ. Some may find the application too stretched in places, but so be it. This is devotional literature in the best Puritan tradition, allowing the illustrations, colours and sounds of the Song to be opened up in the light of the wider Scripture.

Iain D. Campbell,
Minister, Point Free Church of Scotland, Isle of Lewis

Malcolm Maclean has sought to interpret the Song of Songs as a description of Christ and his people rather than as a love song. In doing so, he stands in a distinguished line of biblical interpreters, including James Durham, George Burrowes, Robert Murray M'Cheyne, Alexander Moody Stuart, James Hudson Taylor, and Charles Spurgeon. It must be acknowledged that Ephesians 5:22-33 lends some considerable support to this now largely rejected approach. Even those who are unconvinced by the old approach – and I am one – will find this devotional work rich, powerful, and incisive, and will find it a challenge and a help to their souls.

Peter Barnes,
Pastor, Author, Lecturer,
Revesby Presbyterian Church, Revesby, New South Wales, Australia

The beautiful reality of human married love was always intended by our Creator to be a temporary visual aid to illustrate the eternal love of Christ for the Church (Eph. 5:32). The Song of Songs has traditionally been understood as a glorious exploration of this theme (as well as a lovely depiction of married love). During the twentieth century the evangelical church was profoundly affected in many ways by the surrounding subjective and therapeutic culture, whereby human happiness was regarded as the central end in life. Unsurprisingly the Song of Songs was often reduced to being viewed as a purely human encounter between two lovers. This wonderful book retrieves the Song, unlocking its timeless truths in a way which inspires greater love for Christ and for his Church. It is a powerful reminder of the glory of Christ's matchless love, and provides strong medicine for the soul.

Sharon James,
Conference speaker and author, Leamington Spa, England

A former teacher of mine reminds us how the Song of Solomon comes to us in this world of sin, where lust and passion are on every side, where fierce temptations assail us and try to turn us from the God-given standard of marriage, and this book reminds us, in a particularly beautiful fashion, of how pure and noble true love is. But the God who put this book in the canon of Scripture, has also placed love in the human heart. He is himself pure, and so the Song of Solomon also turns one's eyes to the Lord Jesus Christ. The eye of faith, as it beholds this picture of exalted human love, is reminded constantly of the one love that is above all human affection, that 'love divine all loves excelling' which is the love of the Son of God for the church, his bride. We sing the words, 'From heaven he came and sought her to be his holy bride.' He sought us because he loved us, and he loves us still. Cecil Alexander wrote, 'Oh dearly, dearly has he loved, and we should love him too.' How we should love him for all that he is and all that he has done – with ourselves seeing so small a part of his love. How can we love him more? The Song of Solomon can assist us, and Malcolm Maclean's lucid and warm commentary on the book led me into some royal communion with the King of kings. It will help every Christian reader to rest in his love and say with grander assurance, 'This is my beloved and this is my friend.'

Geoff Thomas,
Pastor, Alfred Place Baptist Church, Aberystwyth, Wales

ROYAL COMPANY

A Devotional on the Song of Solomon

Malcolm MacLean

Malcolm Maclean is Minister of Greyfriars Free Church of Scotland in Inverness, Scotland. Prior to that he pastored the Free Church of Scotland in Island of Scalpay in the Western Isles. Malcolm is also the Editor of the Mentor imprint of Christian Focus Publications and the Free Church of Scotland's magazine *The Monthly Record* has also authored *The Lord's Supper* (ISBN 978-1-84550-428-1).

Unless otherwise indicated, all Scripture quotations are taken from The Holy Bible, English Standard Version, copyright © 2001 by Crossway Bibles, a division of Good News Publishers. Used by permission. All rights reserved."

Scripture quotations marked KJV are taken from the King James Version. All rights reserved.

Scripture quotations marked NKJV are taken from the New King James Version. Copyright © 1982 by Thomas Nelson, Inc. Used by permission. All rights reserved.

Copyright © Malcolm Maclean 2012

ISBN 978-1-84550-718-3

Published in 2012
by
Christian Focus Publications
Geanies House, Fearn, Ross-shire,
IV20 1TW, Scotland

www.christianfocus.com

Cover design by Moose77.com

Printed by Bell and Bain, Glasgow

All rights reserved. No part of this publication may be reproduced, stored in a retrieval system, or transmitted, in any form, by any means, electronic, mechanical, photocopying, recording or otherwise without the prior permission of the publisher or a license permitting restricted copying. In the U.K. such licenses are issued by the Copyright Licensing Agency, Saffron House, 6-10 Kirby Street, London, EC1 8TS www.cla.co.uk.

CONTENTS

Introduction 9

POEM 1: THE SEEKING BELIEVER (1:1-8)
1. The Desire of the Bride Fulfilled (1:1-4) 23
2. A Bruised Saint Seeking Rest from Jesus (1:5-8) 33

POEM 2: IN THE KING'S BANQUETING HOUSE (1:9–2:7)
3. Love's Sweet Greeting (1:9-11) 45
4. The Thoughts of the Bride (1:12-14) 53
5. The Opinion of the King (1:15) 61
6. The Opinion of the Bride (1:16-17) 69
7. Jesus Reveals Himself to His Bride (2:1-2) 77
8. Jesus, the Apple Tree (2:3) 85
9. Jesus, Lover of My Soul (2:4-7) 91

POEM 3: SUMMER IN THE SOUL (2:8-17)
10. The King's Invitation (2:8-13) 101
11. The King's Invitation Answered (2:14-17) 109

POEM 4: LOOKING FOR JESUS (3:1-5)
12. Seeking and Finding the Beloved (3:1-5) 119

POEM 5: THE MARRIAGE JOURNEY (3:6-11)
13. Travelling Together in the City (3:6-11) 127

POEM 6: THE CAPTIVATED KING (4:1–5:1)
14. Christ's Admiration of His People (4:1-7) 137
15. Jesus Is Enthralled by His People (4:8-11) 147
16. The Walled Garden (4:12–5:1) 153

POEM 7: SPIRITUAL RECOVERY (5:2–8:4)
17. The Price of Refusal (5:2-8) 163
18. Love to an Unseen Christ (5:9-16) 171
19. Seeking Jesus Together (6:1-3) 179

20. The King's Opinion of a Restored Backslider (6:4-10) 187
21. The Explanation of the King (6:11-13) 193
22. The King's Appreciation of her Beauty (7:1-9) 201
23. The Restored Disciple's Desire for Fellowship (7:9-13) ... 207
24. The Restored Disciple wants more Fellowship (8:1-4) ... 215

POEM 8: AFTER THE MOUNTAIN TOP (8:5-14)
25. Parting Can be Sweet (8:5-7) 223
26. Commitment (8:8-14) 231
Bibliography 237

Introduction

On 14 August 1836, a young man, who was later to have a remarkable ministry, preached a sermon as a candidate for the position of minister in a new congregation. He chose to expound a passage from the Song of Solomon (2:8-17). His opening words may have startled his audience. Here is what he said:

> There is no book of the Bible which affords a better test of the depth of a man's Christianity than the Song of Solomon. (1) If a man's religion be all in his head – a well-set form of doctrines, built like mason-work, stone above stone, – but exercising no influence upon his heart, this book cannot but offend him; for there are no stiff statements of doctrine here upon which his heartless religion may be built.
>
> (2) Or, if a man's religion be all in his fancy – if, like Pliable in the *Pilgrim's Progress*, he be taken with the outward beauty of Christianity – if, like the seed sown upon the rocky ground, his religion is fixed only in the surface faculties of the mind, while the heart remains rocky and unmoved; though he will relish this book much more than the first man, still there is a mysterious breathing of intimate affection in it, which cannot but stumble and offend him.
>
> (3) But if a man's religion be heart religion – if he hath not only doctrines in his head, but love to Jesus in his heart – if

he hath not only heard and read of the Lord Jesus, but hath felt his need of Him, and been brought to cleave unto Him, as the chiefest among ten thousand, and the altogether lovely, then this book will be inestimably precious to his soul; for it contains the tenderest breathings of the believer's heart towards the Saviour, and the tenderest breathings of the Saviour's heart again towards the believer.'

Who was the young candidate for the ministry and where was the new church? The preacher was Robert Murray McCheyne and the church was St. Peter's in Dundee, Scotland.[1] In fact, during his ministry, which was not very long in terms of years, he would preach from almost every verse in the Song of Solomon.

Others have shared his opinion. C. H. Spurgeon preached about sixty sermons from the Song of Solomon and here and there among them he gives his opinion regarding the value of the Song of Solomon. For example, in a sermon on Song of Solomon 4:10-11, called 'Christ's Estimate of His People', Spurgeon claims that 'The true believer who has lived near to his Master will find this book to be a mass, not of gold merely, for all God's Word is this, but a mass of diamonds sparkling with brightness, and all things thou canst conceive are not to be compared with it for its matchless worth. If I must prefer one book above another, I would prefer some books of the Bible for doctrine, some for experience, some for example, some for teaching, but let me prefer this book above all others for fellowship and communion. When the Christian is nearest to heaven, this is the book he takes with him. There are times when he would leave even the Psalms behind, when standing on the borders of Canaan, when he is in the land of Beulah, and he is just crossing the stream, and can almost see his Beloved through the rifts of the storm-cloud, then it is he can begin to sing Solomon's Song. This is about the only book he could sing in heaven, but for the

---

[1] Andrew A. Bonar (1844, rpt. 1892, 1978), *Memoir and Remains of Robert Murray McCheyne*, Banner of Truth, p. 480.

Introduction

most part, he could sing this through, these still praising him who is his everlasting lover and friend.'

Hudson Taylor, the well-known nineteenth-century missionary to China, had a very high regard for the Song of Solomon and wrote a small exposition of it called *Union and Communion*. In it, he wrote:

> Well may this book be called *the* Song of Songs! There is no song like it. Read aright, it brings a gladness to the heart which is as far beyond the joy of earthly things as heaven is higher than the earth. It has been well said that this is a song which grace alone can teach, and experience alone can learn. Our Saviour, speaking of the union of the branch with the vine, adds, 'These things have I spoken unto you, that My joy might remain in you, and that your joy might be full' (John 15:11, KJV). And the beloved disciple, writing of Him who 'was from the beginning', who 'was with the Father, and was manifested unto us', in order that we might share the fellowship which He enjoyed, also says, 'These things write we unto you, that your joy may be full'(1 John 1:4).
>
> Union with Christ, and abiding in Christ, what do they not secure? Peace, perfect peace; rest, constant rest; answers to all our prayers; victory over all our foes; pure, holy living; ever-increasing fruitfulness. All, all of these are the glad outcome of abiding in Christ. To deepen this union, to make more constant this abiding, is the practical use of this precious Book.'[2]

Going back into the previous century, we find that Jonathan Edwards was helped greatly as a young Christian by meditating on the Song of Solomon. 'From about that time I began to have a new kind of apprehensions and ideas of Christ, and the work of redemption, and the glorious way of salvation by him. An inward, sweet sense of these things, at times, came into my heart; and my soul was led

---

[2] J. Hudson Taylor (1914, rpt, 1996), *Union and Communion*, Christian Focus, p. 13.

away in pleasant views and contemplations of them. And my mind was greatly engaged to spend my time in reading and meditating on Christ, on the beauty and excellency of his person, and the lovely way of salvation by free grace in him. I found no books so delightful to me, as those that treated of these subjects. Those words Cant. ii. 1 used to be abundantly with me, *I am the rose of Sharon, and the lily of the valleys*. The words seemed to me sweetly to represent the loveliness and beauty of Jesus Christ. The whole book of Canticles used to be pleasant to me, and I used to be much in reading it, about that time; and found from time to time an inward sweetness, that would carry me away in my contemplations.'[3]

John Owen is often regarded as the Prince of the Puritans and reading his Collected Works is a major challenge. Yet his writings are full of gold, especially in his insights into the person of Christ and his relationship with his people. In his work on *Communion with God*, as he explains the interaction between Jesus and his people, Owen makes use of the fifth chapter of the Song of Solomon and shows how it reveals, in a marvellous manner, the riches of that relationship. Reading his explanation both extends the mind and enraptures the heart of a believer in love with Jesus.[4]

If these men are right in their assessment of the benefits of using the Song of Solomon in a devotional manner, and they are only a sample of many others who have said the same, then we should spend time reading it and meditating about it. Hopefully, this short book will help you do so, and also to read much fuller treatments (some are mentioned in the short bibliography at the end of the book). It is divided into twenty-six sections, and each of them can be read in a few minutes.

---

[3] *The Works of Jonathan Edwards, Vol. 1*, (1834, rpt. 1974), Banner of Truth, xiii.

[4] 'Communion with God,' *The Works of John Owen*, Vol. 2 (rpt. 1965), Banner of Truth, pp. 71-8.

Introduction

What kind of love story?
It is obvious from the contents of the Song of Solomon that its author refers to a relationship between a man and a woman, which raises the question as to the focus of the book. From the time of the early church fathers down to the beginning of twentieth century, the almost universal opinion among devout commentators was that this book was an allegory depicting the relationship between Christ and his people (either individually or corporately). Today it is common, even among evangelical commentators, to deny that it speaks of that union and instead to claim that it describes the relationship of a husband and wife.

Of course, it is difficult to prove that either view is wrong. Regarding the possibility of a human relationship depicting the tie between Christ and his people, there are other references in the Bible that use the husband/wife union to illustrate the love between Jesus and believers. Paul uses it in Ephesians 5:22-23, John uses it in Revelation 19:6-8 and 21:9ff., the Old Testament prophets use it to describe God and Israel on numerous occasions, it is found in Psalm 45, and Jesus calls himself the Bridegroom (with the implication that his people are his Bride).

It seems to me that sometimes one's interpretation of the Song is connected to one's Christian interests. Some believers are more active than contemplative. It cannot be denied that there is a need for active Christians. But activity, even Christian activity, cannot feed our souls. And I suspect today that there has been a subtle shift from contemplative religion to a form of Christian activism that is commendable in several ways; yet instead of maintaining a balance between a healthy heart religion and a healthy walk, the heart has been largely jettisoned and we have produced a kind of Christianity that is not as warm as the spiritual life of our forefathers. We may be more active in many areas of life, which they may have stayed away from, as we attempt to become light and salt in society. Yet no matter how important these initiatives are, sometimes the cost is too high because they mean that we do not have enough time in which to meet with Jesus Christ and have fellowship with him in our souls.

What has this to do with the Song of Solomon? If it is taken to describe an ideal human marriage, then it ceases to be descriptive of the love between Christ and his people. Perhaps reading the Song as a marriage manual does produce better marriages, although I think that those who do use it in this way reveal as much imagination in interpretation as ever did the allegorists of the past. But is it spiritually wise to remove Jesus from a book of the Bible, especially in face of all the evidence of countless myriads of believers who claim to have met him in the Song of Solomon?

Personally, I think it describes Christ and his people, and taking this approach has been of great blessing to my own heart. I can identify with what Marcus Rainsford wrote in the preface of his own book on the Song of Solomon, 'I can truly say I never expect to enjoy on earth sweeter hours than I spent in the study of this Song of Loves.' Some may respond by suggesting that such an interpretation is subjective rather than objective, as if a subjective experience could not be genuine. This would be a valid criticism if the meanings of the various descriptions in the Song were left to human imagination alone. Yet I would say that using other biblical teachings to prevent illegitimate interpretations also enables a reader to draw appropriate meanings from the descriptions of the King and his beloved in the Song. Surely it is better to have a genuine subjective experience that is in line with objective truth than to have only an objective understanding of a reality. For example, it is good to understand all the details of the truth concerning divine adoption, but it is far better to have that understanding alongside the strong cry of 'Abba, Father,' a subjective experience brought about by the indwelling Holy Spirit.

The Song of Solomon gives to believers an answer to a very important question: 'What is it like to have contact with Jesus Christ?' We make contact with him in a variety of ways. Here are two examples. At times, we come to him as penitent, recovering from inner backsliding – the Song can show us the causes of such spiritual troubles as well as its effects on one's relationship with Jesus, before depicting for us the way of restoration. At other times, we come to Jesus as members of a congregation gathering together to meet with him – the Song, through the contributions of 'the daughters of Jerusalem', describes the joys and delights of fellowship as well as the dangers to such fellowship posed, not by outward enemies, but by friends.

There are many other ways of having contact with Jesus, and we can see them in the Song. Such contact is superior to other encounters that our souls have. For example, on holiday abroad my heart is moved by hearing something related to Scotland (sound of bagpipes, a song played in a shop), but at that moment Scotland does not come to me nor do I have an authentic Scottish experience (merely nostalgia, a substitute for the real thing). Contact with Jesus, however, is genuine because he does, by his Spirit, visit the soul and bring heavenly blessings with him, giving to his lovers tastes of his peace and joy. Since these experiences are not described in such detail elsewhere in the Bible, we need the contents of the Song to guide us as we develop a spiritual relationship with Christ.

Of course, the Song uses the human relationship as a picture, but it is only by illustration that we can speak about God and his ways. The Spirit in the Bible uses many images drawn from human life to depict the ways by which God relates to his people. He is likened to a potter, to a metalworker, to a warrior, to a guide, to a shepherd, to a singer, and many others. All these illustrations depict realities about God. He is the potter who shapes our lives, he is the metalworker who burns off the dross we have accumulated, he is the warrior who fights on our behalf, he is the guide who leads us safely through the desert, he is the shepherd who provides provision, and he is the singer who rejoices over his beloved. Some of these appear also in the Song, although the main illustration is that of a Royal Lover and the woman of his affections. Like the other illustrations, it describes truth in the heart of Christ and depicts his interactions with his people.

Poetry

If you read the book in a modern Bible version, you will see that it is poetry (the version used in this book is the English Standard Version). Poetry is a type of literature that appeals to the imagination; it can draw in illustrations, play on words and introduce an endless manner of ways of depicting a situation.[5] This happens in the Song of Solomon. In one scene, the lovers are in a palace, in another scene they are in a field, in another scene they are on a journey. Poetry is the language of lovers, and it can communicate to our minds in a way that simple prose does not do.

As far as I can tell, there are eight poems within the Song, and they are identified on the contents page. Each of the poems, while able to stand on its own, fits into the overall subject of the Song, which is the relationship between Christ and his people.

I don't think the collection of poems is describing a relationship from its beginning to its conclusion. Rather it contains different pictures or cameos of the relationship believers have with Jesus, highlighting features that recur often in their experience. These features include mutual delight, the effects of spiritual laziness in a believer, the path of spiritual recovery, and longing for perfection.

---

5   'This song sets forth in poetic and dramatic form the subject of subjects, in diverse scenes and personages and experiences; and the whole is arranged as in a many-sided mirror to reflect the beauty and glory of our King, and tell us of his love that passeth knowledge, the love of Christ for me…. A heaven-given riddle, attempting to reveal the love of Christ, and his own Spirit alone can expound it. It may be a detailed history of churches, it is of individual Christian experience, a drop of living water from the ocean of love, a spark of fire from the eternal glory' (Marcus Rainsford [n.d.], *The Song of Solomon*, Simpkin, Marshall, Hamilton and Kent, pp. 7-8).

Introduction

In the main, there are three speakers in the poems: the king, the woman, and the daughters of Jerusalem. The king depicts Jesus, and I take the woman to be a believer and the daughters of Jerusalem to be her fellow-believers. In the original language, usually the speakers can be identified as masculine or feminine, singular or plural, and modern versions of the Bible identify the speakers. The text of the English Standard Version has been included for the help of the user of this book. Occasionally I have departed from its identification of who is speaking in a section of a poem.

The author

The book itself claims to have been written by King Solomon and that claim is sufficient for all who accept the authority of the Bible. It is not known when he wrote the Song of Solomon, but we can deduce from Peter's description of the production of the Old Testament (2 Pet. 1:21) that Solomon would have written the Song when he was in a spiritually-healthy state.

Providentially, the Lord had prepared Solomon to become the author of all his writings. We are familiar with his special request for divine wisdom (1 Kings 3). Regarding the Song of Solomon, through the possession of such wisdom, he was given the ability to compose a poetic masterpiece; further he had the experience of creating palaces, gardens and vineyards (each of which appear in the Song), was familiar with the several aspects connected to each, and so was able to use them wisely as pictorial locations of where to place the characters of the Song as they interact with one another on a spiritual level. His own riches and possessions enabled him to use himself as a picture of Jesus in love with those who are poor in spirit.

It is not difficult to show from Scripture that Solomon is a type of Christ. His names point to Christ: Solomon means 'prince of peace' and he was also called Jedidiah, which means 'beloved of the Lord', because the Lord had special affection for him (2 Sam. 12:24-25). Both these titles, while applicable to Solomon, excel in meaning when he is seen as a type of Jesus, the true Prince of Peace and the eternal Beloved of the Father.

Solomon was also the son of David (the king) who enjoyed the greatest success as far as kingdom building was concerned. While Solomon personally failed to maintain a disciplined walk with God and succumbed to the influence of his pagan wives, his kingdom did become a picture of the future kingdom of the Messiah (for example, Ps. 72, which describes the kingdom of the Messiah, is an enhanced description of Solomon's kingdom).

Could Solomon have written about the Messiah in such an intimate way as revealed in the Song of Solomon? One answer to this question is that he did reveal his interest in the Messianic King by what he wrote in Psalm 72. In that psalm he anticipates the endless and universal reign of the Messiah, one that would be infinitely more durable and extensive that his own reign, great though it was.[6] Since Solomon was guided by the Spirit to describe those more external aspects of the Saviour's kingdom, and to use contemporary illustrations to depict them, why could he not have been guided by the Spirit to describe the greatness of that kingdom from its inner perspective, that of the love between the Messianic King and his subjects, and to use the intimacy of human love to help us appreciate the pleasure of experiencing divine love?

Further, while one cannot say when Solomon wrote the Song, his own experience of departing from God's ways would have given him all the insight he needed for describing the folly of the woman in the Song when she fails to maintain warm affections for the Lover of her soul. There are aspects of the beauty of Jesus that only a restored backslider can appreciate.

---

6 'This psalm agrees with the Song of Songs, in showing that Solomon occupied his mind earnestly with the Messianic kingdom' (E. W. Hengstenberg [1860], 'Prolegomena to the Song of Solomon' in *Commentary on Ecclesiastes and Other Treatises*, Smith, English and Co.,) p. 280.

Introduction

Since there is no reason why Solomon could not have written about the Messiah in an intimate way, we can understand why the title of the Song of Solomon (1:1) indicates that there is something so special about the Song which makes it unique. Solomon wrote over one thousand songs (1 Kings 4:32); he possessed the wisdom that enabled him to make an accurate judgement regarding the differences between them, and this one Song he describes as superior to all the rest. If his assessment was merely based on elegance of style, then it would be possible for him to have written his best song on any topic. But if his assessment was based on the subject of his song, on what greater theme could he written than on the love of Christ for his people? The other songs of Solomon have disappeared (apart from Pss. 72 and 127), and we do not know what was in these missing songs. But we do have his best Song on the best of subjects. That is what divine providence has done with his songs.

The contents of this work began life as a series of sermons preached several years ago in the Scalpay Free Church of Scotland congregation in the Western Isles of Scotland. Sometimes the preaching style will be easily identified. Since they were the first to hear the contents, this book is dedicated to all my friends in the Scalpay Free Church of Scotland, a congregation composed of people who did far more for me than I ever did for them.

Malcolm Maclean
Inverness

POEM 1

THE SEEKING BELIEVER (1:1-8)

She	²Let him kiss me with the kisses of his mouth! For your love is better than wine; ³your anointing oils are fragrant; your name is oil poured out; therefore virgins love you. ⁴Draw me after you; let us run. The king has brought me into his chambers.
Daughters	We will exult and rejoice in you; we will extol your love more than wine; rightly do they love you (Song 1:2-4).

1

The Desire of the Bride Fulfilled

SONG OF SOLOMON 1:1-4

The first poem in the collection opens abruptly, without a reference to where the speakers are located. This means that we have to deduce from their words where they are. One clue is that the woman can smell the fragrance of the king's anointing oils, so obviously he is close by, although out of sight. At first glance, her words could either mean that he had arrived at the place where she is or that she has come to the place where he resides. Verse 4, however, with its reference to her being in the king's chambers, would indicate that she has come to his palace and is walking in the vicinity of his rooms. As she senses his presence, her heart breaks forth into words.

1. The bride prays for reality as opposed to substitutes (v. 2)
'Let him kiss me with the kisses of his mouth.' Some of the early church fathers regarded this desire as the prayer of the Old Testament Church who wanted to get beyond the types and shadows of their era, a desire to move beyond even the predictions of the glorious coming of the Messiah. Such pictures and promises were enough to give them salvation, but what they had been given was only a foretaste or sample of what they knew would yet come. These Old Testament

believers, as they walked throughout the courts of the Old Testament and its means of grace, could smell the perfumes of Christ as he dwelt in his private rooms in heaven.

In a similar manner, we too can be in the king's palace, enjoying the blessings connected with the church. We no longer have types and shadows, and are privileged to have a fuller revelation of the Saviour's purpose and have received clearer promises from him than did the Old Testament believers. This knowledge gives us assurance of our acceptance and his help. Yet there should be in our hearts a longing for more, a desire for intimate reality with our Saviour. When that happens, we are anticipating the experience promised by Jesus in John 14:21: 'Whoever has my commandments and keeps them, he it is who loves me. And he who loves me will be loved by my Father, and I will love him and manifest myself to him.' Like the woman, we want reality in our spiritual experience; when such a desire is present, we will not want a substitute experience, even one that can be described as Christian, because it falls short of meeting with Jesus.

2. The bride prays for repeated displays of affection (v. 2)

She does not merely ask for one kiss, she wants the Lover to embrace her with a multitude of kisses. She is greedy for divine expressions of love. Are there divine kisses in the spiritual life? I will mention two.

First, there is the kiss of *reconciliation*. It was customary for reconciled enemies to embrace once they were brought together. So we can say that a believer, as she senses her need of affection from her Lover, asks him to give her again the sense of being at peace with him. Of course, this experiential embrace of peace is based on the fact that she has already been reconciled to God through faith in Jesus (Rom. 5:1). Yet we know that a country can be at peace with a former enemy without enjoying the fruits of that peace. In a far higher sense, it is possible for believers to have the state of reconciliation without knowing a sense of peace in their hearts. Peace with God in justification should lead on to the peace of God being known in our souls.

A second type of kiss that was found in those days was the kiss of *friendship* or companionship. It was the sign that the other person was delighted to see you and to be with you. The bride wants her Lover to confirm to her that he wants her company. There are scriptures that encourage believers to look for this experience with Jesus. For example, his choice of the apostles had many purposes, but one of them was that they would be with him (Mark 3:14); while this requirement had the meaning of learning from him as disciples by listening to him and observing him, it also revealed his delight in their company. Jesus wanted them to be with him.

Another verse with the same emphasis is Luke 22:15 which contains the words of Jesus to his disciples in the Upper Room when he said to them: 'I have earnestly desired to eat this Passover with you before I suffer.' The Saviour was anticipating abandonment by his Father when on the cross, yet he expressed strongly his deep wish that he spend this special occasion with those he loved sufficiently to die in their place on the cross.

A third example of Jesus' strong desire to be with his people is found in his promise to any person belonging to the backsliding church of Laodicea: 'if anyone hears my voice and opens the door, I will come in to him, and will eat with him and he with me' (Rev. 3:20). What a marvellous promise to the individuals in that church! Using the picture of a visit to a home Jesus desired to spend time with any who would open the door and invite him in.

These sample verses make very clear that one of the activities of a spiritually healthy believer is to look by faith to Jesus for expressions of his delight in his people, even if that believer is in an isolated state, a state that as we have seen can be caused by a variety of reasons.

3. The bride prays from recollection of previous meetings (v. 2)

As the woman thinks about her Lover, she cries, 'For your love is better than wine.' Wine was regarded in the Middle East as a means of bringing joy to a sad heart, of giving strength to a tired heart. A Christian knows that a fresh taste of the love of Jesus will give these blessings to her. Wine symbolises pleasures that bring joy. Getting a tender embrace from Jesus gives more joy to her than all the legitimate pleasures of life. And there is nothing like a fresh embrace from Jesus to revitalise a weary soul, troubled by all the problems caused by the world, the flesh and the devil. When a believer uses these words when speaking to Jesus, she is not speaking second-hand. Rather she has known contacts with Jesus in the past, and these memories will stimulate her to pray for another encounter of love with her Beloved.

Paul stressed the possibility of experiencing the love of Christ in increased ways in his prayer in Ephesians 3:17-19. He prays for his readers 'that Christ may dwell in your hearts through faith – that you, being rooted and grounded in love, may have strength to comprehend with all the saints what is the breadth and length and height and depth, and to know the love of Christ that surpasses knowledge, that you may be filled with all the fullness of God.' He prayed that this would be the experience of all his readers, not merely a select few. Have we prayed this prayer for ourselves? By the Holy Spirit, the love of Jesus can be shed abroad within our hearts as individuals. Have we prayed this prayer for our church? By the Holy Spirit, the love of Jesus can be shed abroad in a congregational meeting as we gather together to interact with him.

4. The bride prays because she has recognised the fragrance of Christ (v. 3)

As was suggested, the picture here is of the woman and her companions walking along a corridor in the king's palace, and as they do the fragrance of the king, there in his private rooms, fills the corridor. As they sense his aroma, the woman affirms, 'Your anointing oils are fragrant; your name is oil poured out; therefore virgins love you.' What is the fulfilment of the corridors of the king's palace in which a lover of Jesus and her friends will sense his fragrances? We can say that they are times of fellowship that believers have in church or in other places. It is a good way to think of church services as corridors in the king's palace, and in each of these services we should smell the fragrance of Christ as he comes to meet with us.

When we think of Jesus, we should remind ourselves that his fragrances are the fruit of the Spirit that he displayed to perfection. Probably the king in the song has been anointed with various oils, a wonderful picture of Jesus anointed with the Holy Spirit. Isaiah mentions some of these aromas in Isaiah 61:1-3: 'The Spirit of the Lord God is upon me, because the Lord has anointed me to bring good news to the poor; he has sent me to bind up the broken-hearted, to proclaim liberty to the captives, and the opening of the prison to those who are bound; to proclaim the year of the Lord's favour, and the day of vengeance of our God; to comfort all who mourn; to grant to those who mourn in Zion – to give them a beautiful headdress instead of ashes, the oil of gladness instead of mourning, the garment of praise instead of a faint spirit; that they may be called oaks of righteousness, the planting of the Lord, that he may be glorified.'

The fragrance of Jesus includes the effects of his beautiful life (a perfect righteousness), of his atoning death (a sacrifice of a sweet-smelling savour), of his possession of the Spirit (not only for himself but also for his people), of his intercession in heaven, and of his coming again.

The woman mentions in particular the fragrance of the king's name. It may be that 'name' is being used here in the sense of character, and that would be a good interpretation because the Saviour's character includes all his perfect attributes such as love, holiness, gentleness and joyfulness. But I wonder if the bride is thinking of the name Solomon itself because the primary fragrance that fills the surroundings is peace, a reminder that the king lives up to his name. And Jesus always lives up to his name. The corridors of his palace, our church services and other times of fellowship, will be marked by peace if Jesus is there. How sad when the corridors are filled with the noxious smell of disagreements and arguments that believers sometimes have among themselves! Or when the nasty odour of denominational pride, or when the offensive stench of individuals strutting about the corridors of his palace, replaces the sweet peace associated with the presence of King Jesus!

Apparently, it was on the occasion of preaching on this verse that John Newton wrote his well-known hymn, 'How Sweet the Name of Jesus Sounds.' Certainly, the believer will find in Christ all that is needed for a fragrant and refreshing life.

> How sweet the Name of Jesus sounds
> In a believer's ear!
> It soothes his sorrows, heals his wounds,
> And drives away his fear.
>
> It makes the wounded spirit whole,
> And calms the troubled breast;
> 'Tis manna to the hungry soul,
> And to the weary, rest.
>
> Dear Name, the Rock on which I build,
> My Shield and Hiding Place,
> My never failing treasury, filled
> With boundless stores of grace!
>
> By Thee my prayers acceptance gain,
> Although with sin defiled;
> Satan accuses me in vain,
> And I am owned a child.

Jesus! my Shepherd, Husband, Friend,
O Prophet, Priest and King,
My Lord, my Life, my Way, my End,
Accept the praise I bring.

Weak is the effort of my heart,
And cold my warmest thought;
But when I see Thee as Thou art,
I'll praise Thee as I ought.

Till then I would Thy love proclaim
With every fleeting breath,
And may the music of Thy Name
Refresh my soul in death!

The woman also notes the type of person who responds with love to the fragrance of the king – the virgins (a description of those who are pure). Whom do they represent? Bernard of Clairveaux suggested this was a reference to angels. No doubt they love Christ as they live in heaven now perfumed by the fragrance of Jesus. Nevertheless the virgins here are the companions of the woman. It is a description of the daughters of Jerusalem and later I will explain why I think they depict all who love Jesus and serve him as they live pure lives.

5. The bride prays because she senses the reception of Christ (v. 4)

The woman, having smelled her Lover's fragrances, senses that he is near. This causes her to cry to him, 'Draw me after you; let us run.' Similarly, as we walk in the corridors of the king's palace, in the services of his church and other places of fellowship, we sense that he is close at hand. When, in a service, we hear about the various fragrances of Jesus these words do not announce a distant Saviour. Rather they are his announcement that he has drawn near.

Each time that happens, we should have the response of the woman. We should pray to Jesus, 'Draw me after you. Don't leave without my having nearer fellowship with you.'

Strangely we often fail in this. We are satisfied with his beautiful fragrances, of discovering that he is near, and don't persevere to get closer to himself.

At the same time, the woman does not forget her companions, but urges them to join her in a closer pursuit of the king ('Let us run,' she says). She knows that she does not have much time, therefore she calls on them to run. Why does she do this? I suppose, firstly, because she knows from previous experience that an occasion lost is gone for ever. Perhaps in the past she has been satisfied with the fragrances and not persevered. She does not want that to recur. This response may not occur in physical life but it certainly occurs in the spiritual life.

Secondly, her response suggests that the heavenly Lover is more likely at times to answer her request when she takes others with her. Often he reveals much of his love to his people, not when they are by themselves, but when they are with other believers to whom he also wants to reveal his love. This is one reason why we should not miss out on gatherings of disciples of Jesus.

The woman's urgent response is met with fulfilment because she next says, 'The king has brought me into his chambers.' This surely is a cry of delight. But it is also an anticipation of discovery because in his chambers she will come to know something of the fullness that the king possesses. And is it not the case that sometimes, in this life, the Saviour takes his people into his private chambers, beyond the corridors as it were, and gives them a special foretaste of heaven. He embraces them with his love, gives them great peace, and their souls are filled with joy.

The answered request of the woman brings great joy to her companions: 'We will exult and rejoice in you; we will extol your love more than wine; rightly do they love you.' They have watched her being embraced by her Lover and they praise him for showing love to her. His goodness to her causes them to resolve to focus on his love, to prize it above all else. Church services are opportunities to display our love for Jesus, and one effect is that other believers will praise him for his response to us. They will affirm with delight the appropriateness of their fellow-Christian loving Jesus and experiencing love from Jesus. Every church service is an occasion for this experience. May we use them as corridors to walk along to the king's private rooms!

She

⁵I am very dark, but lovely,
O daughters of Jerusalem,
like the tents of Kedar,
like the curtains of Solomon.
⁶Do not gaze at me because I am dark,
because the sun has looked upon me.
My mother's sons were angry with me;
they made me keeper of the vineyards,
but my own vineyard I have not kept!
⁷Tell me, you whom my soul loves,
where you pasture your flock,
where you make it lie down at noon;
for why should I be like one who veils herself
beside the flocks of your companions?

Daughters

⁸If you do not know,
O most beautiful among women,
follow in the tracks of the flock,
and pasture your young goats
beside the shepherds' tents (1:5-8).

2

A Bruised Saint Seeking Rest from Jesus

SONG OF SOLOMON 1:5-8

The encounter with the king described in the preceding verses has come to an end because he has left to look after some of his flocks, which is a reminder of the many roles performed by him. In the Song, sometimes he is described as a king, at other times as a shepherd, at other times as a traveller. Similarly the woman is described as performing various tasks: in verse 6 she is a vinedresser, but in verse 8 she is a shepherdess looking after young goats.

The woman in verses 5-7 addresses the two objects of her love: in verses 5 and 6 she speaks to the daughters of Jerusalem and in verse 7 she turns and talks to her Beloved. Here is a picture of Christian fellowship on the horizontal level with God's people and on the vertical level with the Saviour. Her words here are like the words of a believer and not an unconverted person. This is important to note when thinking about how she describes herself.

Her self-assessment (v. 5)
The woman describes herself as black and beautiful simultaneously; her blackness she compares to the tents of Kedar and her beauty she compares to the curtains of

Solomon. Regarding her describing herself as black, there are at least three suggested meanings.

First, the colour of her skin could reveal her origin: she might have come from another country than Israel, which was the homeland of the daughters of Jerusalem to whom she is speaking. Some of the early church fathers suggested these were the words of a Gentile Christian addressing Jewish believers. In any case, they are appropriate words for every Christian, to say that they come from another place that is so different from where they now are. Nevertheless I don't think this is the meaning described here.

A second interpretation is to see the blackness as a reference to indwelling sin and the beauty or comeliness as a reference to the believer's desire for holiness. It is certainly the case that all believers know this twofold assessment of themselves. We can think of the believer in Romans 7 struggling against sin. Paul refers to the inner conflict in a believer when he says that the flesh lusts against the Spirit (Gal. 5:17). This interpretation regards her mentioning of her own vineyard as a confession that she has failed to develop spiritually. Yet I think that she has something else in mind.

The third interpretation takes note that she says that her dark colour was due to being forced to work hard in the heat of the sun – her skin had been burnt and become dry and weather-beaten (like the tents of Kedar). This work was not voluntary, for she likens it to forced labour, to slavery in a dry and barren desert. Her description also indicates that this forced activity occurred in a loveless world – it was her brothers who had caused her bondage. This opposition caused her to neglect her own vineyard.

What is being described here, I think, is the effect of worldly opposition on a child of God. The people of the world, who are related to her by nature, are oppressing her because she is no longer one of them. Vineyards were common in Israel, and were an important source of income. They were places that required hard work to produce the grapes. Those who had them focussed all their energy and interests in them. Vineyards were also places of fellowship and joy; this use is referred to in Micah 4:4: 'But they shall sit every man under his vine and under his fig tree, and no one shall make them afraid, for the mouth of the LORD of hosts has spoken.' When she says that her brothers forced her to work in their vineyards, it is a picture of the world attempting to force a believer to have the same priorities and interests as they do.

This suffering from the world has prevented her from focussing on producing a beautiful place, which I think she had anticipated being a location where she could meet her Beloved. I don't think she means that she has become a backslider – which is often the meaning that is given as an explanation of not keeping her vineyard – because she says that she has kept her beauty despite the opposition.

What comely features does a believer show in times of opposition? There is the grace of perseverance by which he or she continues in the faith; there is the grace of loyalty to a Master whose presence she may not be able to sense; there is the beauty of a broken will by which she submits to her Master's providence; there is the longing for a better world. But there may be a lack of some other graces of the Spirit. For example, Peter says that persecution can cause heaviness instead of joy: 'In this you rejoice, though now for a little while, if necessary, you have been grieved by various trials' (1 Pet. 1:6).

Her request of the daughters of Jerusalem (v. 6)
The harassed believer seems from her own perspective to be a contradiction. This is illustrated by the difference between the black tents of Kedar and the gilded tents of King Solomon that were decorated with jewels. The black tents were weather-beaten and dry, a picture of a believer who needs heavenly refreshment. True, she had some features that resembled the rich possessions of the heavenly Solomon: she was persevering, loyal and dissatisfied with where she was.

But her troubles have prevented her attaining her heart's desire and she is apprehensive that her experience will discourage the people of God. She is concerned that they might think that she is not as fragrant as she should be and assume that she has been disloyal to Jesus.

There is a lesson here about judging other Christians who are going through troubles of soul. Unless they tell us, we cannot see if their soul is going through a desert experience. Opposition can have a draining effect and the last thing a tried believer needs is for fellow believers to stare at the effects of her trials. Don't look at her frailties; instead listen to what she says to her king.

Her request of her Well-Beloved (v. 7)

The daughters of Jerusalem hear an earnest prayer from the harassed woman. As they listen, they discover the aspirations of her heart. Our aspirations give better evidence of our spiritual temperature than do our attainments. The daughters of Jerusalem had not been through a desert experience and seemed content with where they were. In a sense, they were almost like the church in Ephesus with its great attainments, but it was a church with no aspirations after Jesus, a church that the Saviour states had lost its first love (Rev. 2:1-7).

The Christian life has been likened to climbing a mountain. We can imagine a believer who has climbed half-way up. He stops and admires the view and decides that this is a good place to stop. He has understood some deep truths, known some answers to prayer, and made some progress. Sadly he has no aspirations to go higher. But down below him is a believer who does not understand as much as him, who struggles in prayer, and takes one step back for every two steps forward. But she has a desire to reach the top. Which one is the healthier? We are not to judge a person's vision as healthy if all they are seeing is what they saw twenty years ago. And we are not to dismiss a believer who cannot see as much as that person – what is important is that they are seeing more than they did before.

This is an illustration of Paul's teaching in Philippians 3:13-15: 'Brothers, I do not consider that I have made it my own. But one thing I do: forgetting what lies behind and straining forward to what lies ahead, I press on toward the goal for the prize of the upward call of God in Christ Jesus.' And he continues: 'Let those of us who are mature think this way, and if in anything you think otherwise, God will reveal that also to you.' We are not to despise our attainments ('Only let us hold true to what we have attained,' v. 16), but we must have aspirations.

What are the aspirations of the woman? Four can be identified. First, she wants to hear her Beloved's voice. I would take this to be a desire in a Christian for personal communion. It is a request for guidance, but it is for guidance to meet with Jesus.

Second, she speaks out of a heart that is full of love to the king ('You whom my soul loves'). She does not know where he is or why he has allowed her to be harassed (after all, he is the king with total power, so he could have prevented what had occurred to her), but she does know that she loves him. Here is proof that many waters cannot quench love. There are many examples of such love in the Bible regarding God's people. Think of Job as he cries, 'Oh that I knew where I might find him,' (Job 23:3) and listen to him as he says, 'When he has tried me, I shall come out as gold' (Job 23:10). Think of Mary of Bethany after her brother has died. She knows that Jesus could have prevented it ('Lord, if you had been here, my brother would not have died'), but puzzled Mary fell at Jesus' feet because she loved him. There is also Peter who experienced greatly the testing of the world. And when Jesus publicly questioned him about his commitment, he cried out, 'Lord, you know everything; you know that I love you' (John 21:17). Love cannot be alive and well in a backsliding heart, but it is alive and well in a heart that feels dry from desert experiences.

Third, the woman wants strength and rest from her Beloved. No matter how much she loved the daughters of Jerusalem, they could not give her these blessings. Where can she get strength? She knows that she will find it by feeding in the pastures to which he takes his flocks. But where is he? This combination of a sense of weakness and ignorance is often found in believers, and therefore they turn to Jesus for specific guidance about where he strengthens his people. 'The inquiry implies ignorance felt and owned. Nor is it a general indication of the kind of pastures where the shepherd feeds his flock that will suffice his bride, but of the actual pastures into which he is leading them now; not of the places he is wont to frequent, but of the particular spot in which she may at present find him. Such a general direction is all, indeed, that he appears to grant, but is obviously not all that she asks. The inquiry refers to the custom of shepherds guiding their flocks to fresh pastures when one spot has been eaten down, to return thither again when the herbage shall have grown anew. The green pastures of Christ's flock are the whole length and breadth of the Word of God, with all its doctrines, all its ordinances, and all its precepts. Throughout these wide ranges the Good Shepherd leads his flock from place to place, feeding them with food convenient for them. Many of the sheep and not a few of the shepherds overlook this important feature of divine leading; and having fallen on some green spot – it may be the first on which their souls found rest, and haply also the greenest in the wide field of the Word – there they remain, and thence they will not move, though there is now little herbage for them there, and they are feeding on the memory of pastures that once were green. Meanwhile the Shepherd hath gone elsewhere with his flocks, and, thou straying sheep whom he hath restored, it is thy wisdom to ask where he is feeding them now, and where thou mayest find fellowship with him; for "as many as are led by the Spirit of God they are the sons of God".'[1]

---

[1] Alexander Moody Stuart (1857), *The Song of Songs*, James Nisbet, pp. 150-51.

Only Jesus can give them strength, and only Jesus can give them rest. Like the woman when she speaks to the king, believers address Jesus as One experienced in providing such rest, as One who will personally provide such rest, and who can provide rest at the hottest time of the day (noon). As with her, troubles, instead of causing them to despair of help from Jesus, make them more determined to receive help from him. This is an illustration of what Jesus promised in Matthew 11:28-30: 'Come to me, all who labour and are heavy laden, and I will give you rest. Take my yoke upon you, and learn from me, for I am gentle and lowly in heart, and you will find rest for your souls. For my yoke is easy, and my burden is light.' Sometimes, Jesus gives strength and rest simultaneously, at other times he provides special occasions where his followers are given rest without any disturbances.

Fourth, she does not want to have to continually hide the effects of her troubles. If things keep on as they have been, she will have to veil her dark face from her companions. And disciples of Jesus can find themselves in circumstances where they may have to take steps to hide the effects of difficulties from fellow-believers because such effects may discourage them. Copying the woman, they will turn their concerns into prayer.

The response from the daughters of Jerusalem (v. 8)

There is disagreement about who speaks in verse 8, with many suggesting that it is the king and chief shepherd. If that is the case, then what we have here is his estimation of her, which is markedly different from her own assessment. And it is the case that Jesus regards each of his people as beautiful.

Yet I think a case can be made for saying that verse 8 is spoken by the daughters of Jerusalem. The phrase 'O most beautiful among women' also occurs in 5:9 and 6:1, and on both occasions it is spoken by the daughters of Jerusalem. If they are the ones speaking in 1:8, then we see that the opinion fellow believers should have of another believer coping well with difficult situations is that they do not see her faults, but her comeliness. She thought her troubles had made her unattractive, they observed that her problems had not detracted from her beauty. Her fears were groundless.

Advice is given by the daughters as to where to meet the Chief Shepherd: 'If you do not know, O most beautiful among women, follow in the tracks of the flock, and pasture your young goats beside the shepherds' tents.' The way to meet with Jesus is to go where he feeds his people. This picture brings the pastoral imagery of Psalm 23 into mind. It is a similar picture to the corridors of his palace in the previous set of verses, where he reveals himself to his seeking people.

One common temptation for individual believers when things get difficult is for them to avoid meeting with other believers. There may be various reasons for this, such as embarrassment or the attempt to improve oneself before returning to meet with the Lord's people. Yet the best thing a harassed believer can do is go to a church or place of fellowship where Christians are meeting together.

The impression is given that the tracks of the sheep would be easy to find. What are the tracks but the means of grace? Believers in every age have taken the same paths as they made their way through life. In preaching about this detail in the passage, Spurgeon commented: 'Just as the Gospel itself is simple and homely, so is this exhortation and direction for the renewal of communion. It is easy, it is plain. You want to get to Jesus, and you want to bring those under your charge to him. Very well, then, do not seek out a new road, but simply go the way which all other saints have gone. If you want to walk with Jesus, walk where other saints have walked; and if you want to lead others into communion with him, lead them by your example where others have gone.'[2]

There is a wonderful picture of the church here as well – shepherds' tents. These tents would be pitched in a suitable

---

[2] C. H. Spurgeon (rpt., 1996), *The Most Holy Place*, Christian Focus, pp. 99-100.

place, usually near fresh water, which pictures for us a congregation meeting alongside the water of life, the Scriptures. It is from this water that the shepherds (pastors and teachers) draw to refresh weary sheep longing for spiritual provision. And as they receive this provision they find themselves in the presence of the King.

POEM 2

IN THE KING'S BANQUETING HOUSE (1:9–2:7)

The King ⁹I compare you, my love,
to a mare among Pharaoh's chariots.
¹⁰Your cheeks are lovely with ornaments,
your neck with strings of jewels.

Daughters ¹¹We will make for you ornaments of gold,
studded with silver (Song 1:9-11).

3
Love's Sweet Greeting

Song of Solomon 1:9-11

As noted before, the locations in the Song vary. In the previous verses (1:5-8), the location seems to have been in the open fields near to vineyards, with the bride separated from her bridegroom. In this next section the location changes to one of the bridegroom's buildings, with various aspects of their relationship being described until the section closes in 2:7. Chapter 2:4 describes the building as the banqueting house, probably the place where Solomon would entertain his important guests. The picture in this section is that of fellowship and reciprocated love.

No doubt there is a link between the advice given at the end of the previous section and the situation described in these verses. At the end of the previous section, the bride was advised to follow in the footsteps of the flock if she wanted to meet the Shepherd. Since she is now with him, it is evident that she sought him. She is like believers who have discovered their Lover in the public means of grace. We can say it is the public means rather than the private because verse 11 indicates that the daughters of Jerusalem are with her (the use of the plural pronoun 'we').

Notice the way the Bridegroom addresses her – 'my love', a marvellous insight into the heart of Jesus. It was wonderful to observe the desire of grace in a believer's heart when she addressed him as 'the one whom my soul loves'. But it is even more wonderful to listen to his response, 'My love.' It is the language of personal and permanent commitment and delight. Jesus longs for his people much more than they long for him.

The comparison of the Bridegroom

The first point to note is that the Bridegroom has been thinking of his bride and informs her that she is like a mare in Pharaoh's chariots. Today, it would not be complimentary to tell a woman that she looked like a horse, but this was not the case in the ancient world. For example, Helen of Troy was likened to a steed. The image that Solomon has in mind seems to be processions of state when beautifully adorned horses would lead chariots on important occasions. The lead horse in the number of horses was the most outstanding for shape, grace and mobility, and it is to this lead horse that Solomon compares his bride. It may be that he also regards her companions, the daughters of Jerusalem, as the other horses helping to pull the chariot.

Solomon had personal experience of Pharaoh's horses because he traded in them: 'And Solomon's import of horses was from Egypt and Kue, and the king's traders would buy them from Kue for a price. They imported a chariot from Egypt for 600 shekels of silver, and a horse for 150. Likewise through them these were exported to all the kings of the Hittites and the kings of Syria' (2 Chron. 1:16-17).

What does this description mean when applied to the believer? I would make five suggestions.

Their purchase

First, his description is a reminder that Jesus was prepared to pay a high price for his people. The passage in 2 Chronicles tells us that Solomon paid a large amount for Egyptian horses. Of course, there is one major difference. The horses that Solomon bought were the best that money could buy. This could not be said of Christians when Jesus ransomed them from the power of sin. They were not only captives of the devil and enslaved to their lusts – they were also in the prison house of God's condemnation, waiting for the execution to be carried out.

Further, it is unlikely that Solomon himself would have journeyed to Egypt to personally purchase the horses; he would have sent a suitable agent. But it was different with Jesus. He could not send an agent, because there was no agent, not even in heaven, who could do this apart from himself.

Again, purchasing the horses would not have brought Solomon into poverty. They were only a small part of his possessions and indeed he sold most of them to other rulers. With Jesus, it was different. The price for redeeming his people was so costly that the apostle Paul says that Jesus became poor (2 Cor. 8:9). He became poverty-stricken as he gave up, for a season, his privileges and rights.

As Solomon looked on the horses he had purchased, he was pleased with them. But his pleasure is nothing compared to the delight of the Son of God. It was his eternal desire to come and deliver his people from the state of condemnation. With great joy he became a man and with great determination and resolve he went to the cross of Calvary in spite of the terror that awaited him there. He gladly paid the price of their redemption.

Their training

Second, the horses that Solomon used in his chariots would have undergone prolonged periods of training until they were fit to pull his chariots. It is the same with the people of Christ. They are the disciples of the Master. Again there is a difference between Solomon and Jesus because I think it is unlikely that Solomon would have been involved in personally training the horses. But Jesus is involved in training each of his people to serve him. He refers to this role in Matthew 11:28-30: 'Come to me, all who labour and are heavy laden, and I will give you rest. Take my yoke upon you, and learn from me, for I am gentle and lowly in heart, and you will find rest for your souls. For my yoke is easy, and my burden is light.'

Sometimes the training of Solomon's horses would be more severe because their rebellious wills would have to be tamed. And a similar kind of instruction is occasionally given to Christ's disciples because of their lack of devotion or because of their worldliness. And it is Jesus who personally applies the correction, as he indicated to the church in Laodicea: 'Those whom I love, I reprove and discipline, so be zealous and repent' (Rev. 3:19). Such occasions are not pleasant (for Jesus or for his people), but they are profitable for Christians. As the writer to the Hebrews says: 'For the moment all discipline seems painful rather than pleasant, but later it yields the peaceful fruit of righteousness to those who have been trained by it' (Heb. 12:11). We saw an example of this training in the previous section in the Song when the woman was harassed and persecuted by her natural brothers. Despite their actions, she had retained her beauty; indeed she had developed it. Christ trains his people so that they will look their best for him.

Their development
Thirdly, following on from the need of training is the fact that the horses of Solomon would have needed to develop strength and energy. The way this would happen is by good food and plenty exercise. Similarly, Christians need good spiritual food and ample spiritual exercise. The food they need is the Word of God and the best way of digesting it is by meditation. They eat it by personal reading of the Scriptures and by listening to expositions of it. The exercise in which

they engage is obedience to God's commandments. These are the signs of a healthy Christian.

But the image of a horse reminds us of another aspect of the Christian life. Believers are compared to many creatures in the Bible. In Isaiah 40, they are likened to soaring eagles; they are also compared to doves and pelicans in the desert by the psalmists. Probably the most common allusion is that of sheep, and it describes features such as docility, weakness and need of constant care. But the image of horses and chariots reminds us that believers are also called to be soldiers in a war against the powers of darkness. And they receive strength for this conflict from the Word of God and by obedience to his Word. This reception of strength is seen in the Saviour's own temptations by the devil; Jesus stated that man must live by every word that proceeds from God and defeated the devil by obeying God. Similarly, believers become strong when the word of God abides in them and then they overcome the wicked one (1 John 2:14).

Their task

Fourthly, the other use, in addition to warfare, of horses and chariots was on grand state occasions when the king would appear publicly in splendour. It is also the case that Jesus desires that his people appear in public in a beautiful manner. Obviously, in this regard we can think of the great triumphant procession at the Saviour's return that will march down the streets of the celestial city when all the redeemed parade in victory. It will be a wonderful sight, as they are admired by the heavenly host and they observe the beauty that Jesus has given them.

Yet there is also another application, which is that believers pull the chariot of Jesus day by day. At present, the chariot is invisible to the world but the horses are not. The world should see beautiful believers and then sense the presence of the invisible Charioteer with them. We can say that where there are Christians being beautified, Jesus is not far behind them. But if a Christian is not being beautified, it may be that he has slipped the reins and is in need of more training.

Their togetherness
Fifthly, also connected to the above is the obvious need for the horses pulling the chariot to do so in harmony. This is a reminder that the woman in the Song needs to get along with the daughters of Jerusalem, that each believer has to work in concord with others who are serving the Master. This emphasis on corporateness was also seen in the previous section in the Song where the woman was told that she would find her Beloved when she followed along with the flock. It does not take much imagination to know that a team of horses which acted independently and tried to go in different directions simultaneously would not get very far. In fact they would not get anywhere because they are tied together, but they would manage to inflict some bruises and kicks on one another. The same thing happens in local congregations of Jesus when each believer does not obey the Master.

All these details are evidence of his love for her, so as he went through each of these experiences on her behalf he was addressing her as 'My love'. When he redeemed her, he said, 'My love'; when he trains her, he says, 'My love'; when he strengthens her, he says, 'My love'; when he parades her in public, he says, 'My love'; when they are in harmony, he says, 'My love.' In each of them, they would experience 'Love's Sweet Greeting' from Jesus.

Because of these experiences, the Beloved can see the beauty that has come to his bride: 'Your cheeks are lovely with ornaments, your neck with strings of jewels.' She is indeed a suitable wife for the king; her beauty is beyond price.

But I will close this meditation by noting the response of the daughters of Jerusalem in verse 11: 'We will make for you ornaments of gold, studded with silver.' What does this mean? The companions of the woman dedicate themselves to keep her beautiful. Is that not a lovely picture of a church or a group of believers? Of course, they can only do so by living in the Spirit. Paul refers to one way of doing this in Ephesians 4:29: 'Let no corrupting talk come out of your mouths, but only such as is good for building up, as fits the occasion, that it may give grace to those who hear.' There are many other such verses concerning building one another up. But this declaration of the daughters of Jerusalem was also, in the ears of the bride, 'Love's Sweet Greeting.'

Perhaps it will be asked, 'Does this mean that part of a believer's beauty is provided by someone in addition to Christ?' The answer is no because even when other believers help a Christian in the development of sanctification (which can be called becoming beautiful and Christlike), they are guided and enabled to do so by the Spirit. Jesus is providing them with all their beauty, but he provides aspects of it in different ways. Sometimes he does it through what is said in a sermon; at other times he uses what is said at a Bible Study or time of fellowship; he may use a word of encouragement or he may use a word of rebuke of other Christians to bring beauty to one of his sheep. And when they say such things, their words are 'Love's Sweet Greeting.'

She   ¹²While the king was on his couch,
my nard gave forth its fragrance.
¹³My beloved is to me a sachet of myrrh
that lies between my breasts.
¹⁴My beloved is to me a cluster of henna blossoms
in the vineyards of Engedi (1:12-14).

4

The Thoughts of the Bride

Song of Solomon 1:12-14

These verses continue the dialogue that began in 1:9 and continues down until 2:7. The location is the banqueting house in one of Solomon's buildings. The woman's thoughts are detailed in verses 12 to 14. In these verses she is not speaking to the king (he is described in the third person and not in the second). It is possible that she is speaking to the daughters of Jerusalem (although unlikely, for she seems to be speaking to herself). Speaking to oneself is a biblical description of meditation (Ps. 1:2). In her meditating, she reminds herself of where she is (at a table) and with whom she is (the king). If she is speaking to the daughters of Jerusalem, then what we have here is another picture of fellowship.

Some comments can be made about the translation of these verses. Verse 12 is straightforward; modern translations differ from the Authorised Version regarding the second clause of verse 13 ('he shall lie all night betwixt my breasts'), and I think correctly. For example, the words 'all night' are not in the original text and were added by the translators because of how they translated the clause. (Spurgeon, in a sermon on verse 13, comments that a believer does not only want Christ during the night, he or she also wants him during the day.)[1] It is more likely that the reference is not to the king lying between her breasts but to a small bottle of myrrh being placed there. She is likening the king's presence to this fragrance that she placed on that part of her body.

Note first, the posture of the king. He is sitting with her at his table. And we can say that Jesus provides a table for his people in all kinds of situations. In Psalm 23, the writer states that he even provides a table in the midst of his enemies. The table is a picture of lifelong fellowship. Sitting at a table is a wonderful picture of communion, of contentment, of delight. She observes that the king is delighted to be there with her. This was in contrast to the sad feature that Jesus the King discovered about the church in Laodicea; although he wanted to sup with her, she did not wish to sit with him (Rev. 3:20).

Note second, the provision on the table. The range of dishes has been provided by the king. In the imagery both he and she feed on the same menu. As we think of Jesus and his people, we should identify matters of common interest that gives them mutual delight. There are a limitless number of courses in this meal. One course could be the attributes of God, another course could be the purposes of God, and still another course could be the promises of God. And within each course itself, there are a variety of dishes – for example, how many dishes could one find in the course called the promises of God? Further, at this table, we can eat our fill.

As the king and the woman eat together, her fragrance is noticeable. This seems to be a picture of the fruit of the Spirit, these beautiful features that give beauty to a Christian. It is not too much to say that each course on the table stimulates these features, with the result that increasing fragrance envelops the atmosphere. As they think about and feed on God's attributes, purposes and promises, her love, joy, peace,

---

1   C. H. Spurgeon (1996), pp. 114-15.

The Thoughts of the Bride

gentleness etc. increase and bring delight to his heart. And, of course, the 'presence of Christ draws forth every grace that is in the believer. Repentance, faith, hope, love, gratitude, joy, peace, which had lain cold and frozen in his absence, are now drawn out toward him as to the source whence they had all flowed.'[2]

Note thirdly, the priority of her heart which is revealed in her description of the king when she likens him to the sachet or bottle of myrrh that she had between her breasts and to a cluster of camphire from Engedi. In order to see the point of her description, we need to see how myrrh was used in the ancient world and to note the location of Engedi.

The use of myrrh (v. 13)

There at least five uses of myrrh that can help us understand its relevance to a relationship between a believer and Jesus. First, myrrh was a very costly fragrance, often worth more than its weight in gold, and this points to the exceeding value of Jesus Christ. Who can calculate what he is worth?

Second, myrrh was a preserving fragrance because it was used in the embalming of dead bodies. For example, it was used by Nicodemus and Joseph to anoint the dead body of the Saviour (normally about eleven pounds was used on a person; they used a hundred pounds on Jesus, so indicating how much they loved him). As we think of the preserving function of myrrh, it is a reminder that it is the presence of Jesus in the soul that prevents it from decaying.

Third, myrrh had many medicinal uses. In the ancient world it was used for cleaning wounds and sores. Even in the nineteenth century it was used to treat coughs, colds, sore throats, bad breath, gum disease, and other health problems. It is a common ingredient in toothpaste. In John Bunyan's classic book, *Pilgrim's Progress*, a bundle of myrrh was used to

---

2 Alexander Moody Stuart (1857), p. 176.

prevent Mercy from fainting. And myrrh was given to Jesus on the cross as a kind of analgesic to dull the pain of crucifixion. As far as believers are concerned, Jesus is the only Physician who can heal their wounds.

Fourth, myrrh overpowered other odours that were in the room. One usage of myrrh was in the Jewish sacrificial system where it was used to counterbalance the smell of burning animals. Sadly, we can find noxious smells as well as other aromas in this world. Therefore we need a more powerful fragrance that will remove them. Nothing gets rid of the smell of sin as the fragrance of Christ.

Fifth, myrrh had to be crushed in order to give out its fragrance. We can see this idea in the letter to the church at Smyrna (Rev. 2:8-11), which is a name connected to myrrh. That church was going to be crushed by persecution, but when the ten days of trouble came, the church would give a sweet aroma to God. In a far greater way, Jesus had to be crushed in order to give out his fragrance.

Psalm 45 is a prophecy of Christ on his future wedding day and he is depicted as being clothed in garments fragrant with myrrh and aloes and cassia (v. 8). His wedding day will be the future resurrection day, when Jesus will show his preserving ability by raising his people from the state of death and his medical ability by healing completely all their diseases. As we see him on that day fragrant with myrrh, we will understand as never before how valuable he is. Yet although he will be glorious, we will also see the evidence of the fact that he once was crushed, when we see the wounds on his body.

The location of Engedi (v. 14)
The king is also compared to a cluster of camphire in the vineyards of Engedi. The camphire is a tall plant (eight feet) with a striking flower (combination of white and yellow), that grows in dense clusters, gives a beautiful fragrance,

and which women used to carry in their hands or in their bosom. Its trunk was cut open in order to obtain material from which perfume was made. So its usage was similar to myrrh, designed to make the wearer fragrant.

But the poet, in a manner common to Hebrew poetry, enhances his meaning in the next line, and does so by mentioning Engedi. Engedi is an oasis in the Judean desert near to the Dead Sea, where enough water pours down from a spring, six hundred feet up in the rocks, in such abundance for several vineyards to be located there. Engedi is a symbol of life in an environment of death.

I don't think it is too difficult to state that the bride sees herself to be in an environment of spiritual death, namely, the world. Yet she is so thankful that in this spiritual desert there is an oasis, which, like Engedi, is filled by water that flows down from above. That oasis is Jesus and he is full of the water of life.

To hold in one's hand or wear in one's bosom the camphires of Engedi is to wear fragrance that has its source in another world. But into this lifeless world comes, through the torn side of Jesus, refreshing fragrance for our dry souls.

Wearing the bundle of myrrh and clusters of camphires

Those who wear the bundle of myrrh and the camphires of Engedi stand out from the crowd. In Song 3:6 the question is asked, 'Who is this coming out of the wilderness like pillars of smoke, perfumed with myrrh and frankincense, with all the merchant's fragrant powders?' (NKJV) This is a picture of the church journeying through the desert to Canaan. What are observable about her are her prayers (incense) and her fragrance (myrrh and frankincense). She is distinctive.

Those who wear the bundle of myrrh and the camphires of Engedi give out a fragrance of Christ. Their presence should have the same effect as if Jesus had been there.

There is a simple poem written by an unknown author that sums this up:

> Not only by the words we say,
> Not only by our deeds confessed,
> But in a most unconscious way
> Is Christ expressed.
>
> For me, 'twas not the truth you taught,
> To you so clear, to me so dim;
> But when you came to me
> You brought a glimpse of Him.
>
> And from your eyes He beckoned me,
> And from your heart, His love was shed,
> 'Til I lost sight of you
> And saw the Christ instead.

The imagery of a bottle of myrrh and a cluster of camphire reminds us that we should have a great abundance of Christ. It is not a drop of myrrh or a solitary flower that the woman puts in her bosom. There is no bottle in the world that can hold all of Christ, but neither is there any reason why our bottles should not be full. Fill up the bottles with the various features that belong to Jesus. Have in the bottles the many promises he made, the peace he gives, the pardon he bestows, the repentance he gives, and many other features. When they will be present, there will indeed be a beautiful aroma.

Further, the contents of the bottle should always be fresh. Of course, Jesus never becomes stale. But sometimes the contents we have are only what Jesus did for us in the past. If we can change the metaphor, our spiritual lives can be like a photograph album in which we have pictures of when we looked better, when we were thinner or had more hair, reminding us of times that we wish could come again. Instead of being like a photograph album from the past, our spiritual lives should be like a live film, where spiritual beauty and Christlikeness can be seen. We should take our bottles and fill them continually with Christ.

The king   Behold, you are beautiful, my love;
           behold, you are beautiful;
           your eyes are doves (1:15).

5
The Opinion of the King

Song of Solomon 1:15

As we noticed previously, we are in a section or poem in which the king and the bride are depicted as sitting in his banqueting house admiring one another. James Durham describes this interaction as a 'holy contest of love'. They are not alone because the daughters of Jerusalem are there as companions, not just of the bride but also of the king.

The king here is responding to the bride's expression of affection in verses 12 to 14. It was suggested in the previous chapter that her description was probably the thoughts of personal meditation or else words expressed to the daughters of Jerusalem. As far the words of the king are concerned, they could be a response to either activity. Such practices by Christians, whether individual meditation on Christ or corporate discussion about Christ, always lead to a divine response.

Take a couple of examples from the Bible. One is from the backslidden days in which Malachi the prophet lived. The response of the godly was to have fellowship, and Malachi 3:16 states that 'those who feared the Lord spoke with one another. The Lord paid attention and heard them, and a book of remembrance was written before him of those who feared the Lord and esteemed his name.' The Lord was pleased with their fellowship. Another example is the words of Jesus in John 14:21: 'Whoever has my commandments and keeps them, he it is who loves me. And he who loves me will be loved by my Father, and I will love him and manifest myself to him.' This verse details the response of Jesus to a person who loves him.

In this verse in the Song of Solomon, the king gives his estimation of his bride and tells her that she is *all* fair before focussing on one particular feature of her appearance, her eyes. But the verse also reveals his earnestness in wanting her to know how he regards her because he repeats his estimation of her. Perhaps he sensed her reticence in not speaking directly to him in the previous verses and he wants to encourage her to engage directly with him.

The king's attitude here illustrates the matter of assurance. In the past, the means of assurance have been likened to a three-legged seat. One leg that provides assurance is the promises in the Bible that, for example, tell sinners that they will be saved as soon as they believe in Jesus. The second leg is the evidence of a changed life: new desires, new activities, and new friends. It is not possible to have assurance without these two legs. Yet it is possible for the stool to balance on two legs, although very unsteadily. The third leg provides strength to assurance and enables a believer to hold his balance through all the spiritual storms that come along. This third leg is usually called the witness of the Spirit and it can occur in a variety of ways, one of which is visits by the Saviour to the hearts of his people.

First of all, we should note the title by which the king addresses the woman: 'my love.' As we think of Jesus' love to each of his people, we recall that it is an *eternal* love, a love that was always in his divine heart. Further, it was an *engaging* love in the sense that he committed himself to deliver each of his people from their sins when

The Opinion of the King

he received them in the covenant of redemption as a love gift from his Father. It was also an *expiating* love because its activity demanded that he atone for their sins. And it was an *entreating* love as he came near their souls in their unconverted days, drawing them to himself through the gospel. His entreating love became an *enabling* love when, by the Holy Spirit, he caused them to embrace him freely and gladly. And this love is an *eager* love for their fellowship that continues all through their journey on earth, despite their sins and shortcomings. And his love causes him to desire to *express* it as often as possible, which is what he is doing here.

Second, the king stresses that he sees no ugliness in her. This is like Jesus stressing to his disciple that he sees no defilement in her. She is fair because she is clothed with the garments of his righteousness, imputed to her permanently when she believed in him for salvation. She is fair because she is clothed with the garments of sanctification and is becoming holy in heart and life, even if she is blind to her progress. And she is fair in her prospects because one day she will be perfect in holiness.

An illustration may help us understand how Jesus can see her as fair even although she is still sinful. We can imagine a man who comes down to visit his girlfriend because he loves her. She is down at their new home, attempting to get it ready for their wedding. When he arrives at the house, she is working in the garden trying to get rid of the weeds by using the tools he has provided her with. But the work has made her dirty and tired. Does her current state make him love her less? No! Because he loves her he goes and helps her clean up the garden and his presence gives her more strength. It is the same with Christ and his people: the garden is her heart and life where he is to dwell for ever; the tools are the Bible and the means of grace that he has given to her; his presence becomes real by the power of the Spirit who cleanses her by the Word at the same time as he strengthens her for more work. And through it all, he is expressing his love for her.

What a surprising statement from Jesus, that the one he loves is all fair! But what a wonderful and comforting statement of the omniscient Saviour!

Third, we can note the significance of the king mentioning her eyes. This is a picture of how Jesus likes to consider the individual graces of his people. We sometimes think that some graces are more prominent than others in believers. For example, John is called the apostle of love and Peter is regarded as a more active believer. While the character traits of an individual may cause some graces to be more obvious, we should not think that other graces are not there. John was also marked by obedience and Peter loved the Lord.

It is a marvellous thought to ponder that Jesus delights to consider the individual graces in his people. We can take the biblical lists of these graces, such as the Beatitudes or the fruit of the Spirit, and run through them, saying to ourselves, 'Jesus looks for life here.' Here the particular aspect he considers is the dove-like sight of his people. What can be said of doves?

First, a dove *mourns*. Hezekiah, in his response to the prophetic message that he would die, said that he mourned like a dove (Isa. 38:14). The people of Israel in their distress likened themselves to doves in Isaiah 59:11: 'We all growl like bears; we moan and moan like doves; we hope for justice, but there is none; for salvation, but it is far from us.' There are many things that make a believer mourn: personal failings, sins of society, backsliding in the church. It is appropriate for a believer to be like a dove and have a tear in his eye. The dovelike spirit of a Christian is a penitent one that leads him to confess his sins.

The Opinion of the King

Second, a dove was a symbol of *purity*. One reason was its white colour. Also, when the flood was over, Noah sent out two birds, a dove and a raven. The raven did not return because it could feed on carrion floating on the water. The dove was different because she could not eat dead things. Similarly a dovelike Christian has a diet that is marked by purity.

Third, a dove is a symbol of *peace*. Jesus mentions this feature when he tells his disciples to be 'wise as serpents, and harmless as doves' (Matt. 10:16). Linked to this is the concept of gentleness. Christians know the peace of God in their hearts, they have a message of peace, and they are to do the things that make for peace.

Fourth, a dove's song was *a sign of spring*, of the return of the period of life after the death of winter: 'The flowers appear on the earth, the time of singing has come, and the voice of the turtledove is heard in our land' (Song 2:12). The Christians' song is a sign of life in this world of death, that there is yet to be a springtime. This will take place at the resurrection, and that spring will lead into an eternal summer. This is a good way for Christians to regard one another, as God-given signs of the future world that is marked by the fullness of eternal life.

Marked by a sense of penitence, a desire for purity, and a longing for peace, the Christian opens his or her eyes to where these blessings can be obtained. A dove's eyes are noted for their clear-sightedness; they can see a crumb on the ground in a public square full of people. And the eyes of the souls of dovelike Christians know where to look when they want increased penitence, purity and peace. They are found in Jesus. Penitence for their sins flows not so much from gazing at their sins but from looking at the Saviour who suffered for these sins. Purity comes by considering the beautiful person of Jesus Christ. Peace comes from fellowship with Christ.

As the Christian opens his eyes to look at Jesus, Jesus observes the direction of the look. And he is delighted when by faith they look straight at him. Their sight goes beyond the visible and sees Christ in all the range of his activities. Their vision extends to where Christ is, and they see him in creation, providence, in the means of grace, in the Bible.

The consequence for a believer of looking at Jesus is increasing Christlikeness. Of the king in this song it is also said: 'His eyes are like doves beside streams of water, bathed in milk, sitting beside a full pool' (5:12). The four details that were mentioned about the dove are also true of Jesus: sorrow for sin, purity, peace, and sign of the coming spring. Of course, Jesus did not repent of personal sins because he did not have any. But he was still saddened by sin in the lives of others and in its effects. Jesus loves holiness, and this should be a primary motive in leading us not to engage in sinful practices. Jesus furthers peace by bringing sinners to himself through the gospel and by dealing with them gently as his people. And Jesus is the Sign of the coming Springtime when once again the world will be beautiful and fair.

As the Christian opens his eyes like a dove, he gives proof that the Heavenly Dove has been at work in his heart. The Holy Spirit descended as a dove on the Saviour when he was baptised. Like the Son, the Spirit too has the four features just mentioned. He convicts us of our sins because he is grieved by them; he loves holiness, indeed it is one of his titles; he furthers peace by bringing to us the peace of God; and he is the first fruits and guarantee of the future glory.

There is another feature that the Bible mentions about doves: they are defenceless (Ps. 74:19: 'Do not deliver the soul of your dove to the wild beasts; do not forget the life of your poor forever'). But Jesus knows that his people are defenceless. Nevertheless, it is a powerful plea to make in prayer, that the Saviour's doves are surrounded by fierce enemies. To the features of penitence, purity, peacefulness and prospect, we must add the necessity of dependant prayer to the character of a dove-like Christian.

She   ¹⁶Behold, you are beautiful, my beloved, truly delightful.
Our couch is green;
¹⁷the beams of our house are cedar;
our rafters are pine (Song 1:16-17).

6

The Opinion of the Bride

Song of Solomon 1:16-17

As we have noted, the section of the Song from 1:9–2:7 is set in one of the king's banqueting houses in which the king and his bride, along with the daughters of Jerusalem, are speaking about their mutual affection. In verses 16 and 17, the king and his beloved appear to have moved outside the building and are in the palace gardens where there would be lawns, trees and flowers. The next few verses are connected to different flowers and trees seen in the garden before the couple return to the banqueting house in 2:4. In addition to grass and cedar and fir trees, the couple refer to roses, lilies, and apple trees. What this points to is the wonderful variety of places and ways in which Christ has fellowship with his people.

As we look at this statement of the bride, we should note, firstly, that it is made in *response* to his words of love. He had described her as doubly fair and the object of his love. It is similar with regard to Jesus. His love is first, in the sense that it is *eternal*, which is why the apostle John says in 1 John 4:19: 'We love, because he first loved us.' But his love should be first *experientially* as well, although it should set off a chain of reciprocal statements.

How do we obtain this experiential love of Jesus? I suspect the best way is to read his love letters. We can imagine a couple separated from each other for a time because the husband is in the army or in work overseas. The husband sends letters to his wife in which he expresses his thoughts of her, and as she reads them his words warm and stir up her affections. So it is with the Bible; it contains Jesus' expressions of love. The illustration falls short in that there is a distance between the husband and the wife; the gap between Jesus and his people is bridged by the Spirit of Jesus who brings fresh experiences of Christ's love to them. But these experiences come through the teachings of Scripture being read, or meditated on, or preached about.

Secondly, we can see that her response indicates that she does not primarily delight in his description of her. He had commented on her dovelike eyes, which from a Christian point of view is a description of her sanctification. No doubt, his words were a wonderful means of assurance for her, yet she places no confidence in her Christian progress. Essential as sanctification is, and important for us to discern it, when we are in the Saviour's presence we should speak about him. Let him speak about us, and his voice is sweet and good to hear. But let us speak about him because he is our only hope.

Thirdly, I would suggest that the act of faith that looks away to Jesus has the companion grace of repentance. The bride knows that her sanctification, although a divine work, is imperfect and therefore she looks to her Beloved with gratitude because his perfection makes up for her imperfection.

The description she gives (v. 16)

First, we should observe the title by which she addresses him – 'my Beloved.' This is a term of very strong endearment, an expression of her devotion and her love. Her words are suitable for a believer to use regarding Jesus. He has captured her heart, but she also realises that it is appropriate for her to speak to him about her feelings. She sings with the psalmist, 'I love the Lord' (Ps. 116:1); she confesses with Peter, 'Lord, you know all things; you know that I love you' (John 21:17, NKJV).

Then she describes her Beloved as fair and pleasant. In what ways is Jesus fair? There are several ways in which this question can be answered. One way is to say that he is perfect in the same graces as she possesses in imperfection. She can look at her King and see in him the fullness of the fruit of the Spirit. In Jesus, to perfection, are seen the graces of love, joy, peace, patience, kindness, goodness, faithfulness, gentleness and self-control. Her admiration of these features will increase as she sees them revealed in him in his Word. We can take the incidents and parables in the Gospels involving the Saviour and admire these aspects of his character.

Another way of stating his fairness is to describe his features as the eternal Son. Jesus was infinite, eternal and unchangeable in his being, wisdom, power, holiness, justice, goodness and truth. When we look at his attitudes in the Trinity we see great beauty in him because of his perfection within the Godhead. And as we listen in to their eternal counsels, we see beauty in his willingness to become the sin-bearer, and in the way each member of the Trinity focussed on the plan of salvation.

Then he was fair in his coming to earth when he added a human nature to his divine Person and became God and man, in two distinct natures and one person for ever. It is a marvellous sight to consider, the unity of the two natures in the one Person of Jesus. He was fair in the cradle, he was fair in the carpenter's shop, he was fair among the crowds during his public ministry, he was fair in his compassion on the multitudes and on individuals, and he was fair in his obedience to God's law throughout his life. Even more so, he was fair on the cross, although he was bloodied and bruised in body and soul, as he paid the penalty for sin. Certainly, he was fair on the resurrection morning as he came out of the tomb, with his beautiful wounds still on his body. Surely, he is fair today exalted to the throne of God. And he will be fair when he returns for his church in the future.

Yet to say something is fair is slightly different from saying it is pleasant. We could say that 'fair' is an objective observation and 'pleasant' is a subjective observation. James Durham distinguishes them by suggesting that *pleasant* points to 'their actual feeding upon the beautiful sight they have gotten of him'.[1] All these aspects of his beauty that we have mentioned need to be tasted personally in order for them to become pleasant. An illustration may be this: imagine the difference between a painting of a beautiful meal and the eating of the same meal. All who look at the painting can say it looks beautiful, but only those who eat it can say it is pleasant. Pleasant is connected to pleasure and delight, and when Jesus by the Spirit becomes intimately involved with us, individually or corporately, we will say that he is pleasant.

Every believer can say about Jesus, who is full of the fruit of the Spirit, that he is the Fountain out of which he gives graces to each of them. Every believer can say about Jesus, the eternal Son, that he thought of each of them in that eternal covenant; indeed he was thinking about each of them throughout that unbeginning eternal

---

1   James Durham (1840, rpt. 1997), *The Song of Solomon*, Banner of Truth, p. 122.

day. Each believer can go through every action of Jesus recorded in the Gospels, including his death, and say it was done for him or her. Each believer can stand with the disciples outside the empty tomb and say that 'He rose for me, he is ascended for me, and he is coming for me.' This is what makes his fairness pleasant.

> Jesus, my Saviour, to Bethlehem came,
> Born in a manger to sorrow and shame;
> Oh, it was wonderful, blest be his Name,
> Seeking for me, for me.
>
> Jesus, my Saviour, on Calvary's tree,
> Paid my great debt and my soul he set free,
> Oh, it was wonderful, how could it be,
> Dying for me, for me.
>
> Jesus, my Saviour, the same as of old,
> While I did wander afar from the fold,
> Gently and long did he plead with my soul,
> Calling for me, for me.
>
> Jesus, my Saviour, will come from on high,
> Sweet is the promise as weary years fly;
> Oh, I shall see Him descending the sky,
> Coming for me, for me.

Shares his possessions (vv. 16-17)

As mentioned earlier, I think the imagery in 1:16-17 is taken from the trees and flowers and lawns that were in the king's gardens. They were places of refreshment and rest where the king and his friends would retire to for moments of peace and recovery, similar to an oasis in the desert or the still waters in a mountainous area. In particular, they were suitable havens in a country of great heat. They are his possessions, which he gladly shares with his bride. Perhaps they are sitting on the grass, looking up to the strong cedars and firs.

Of what is this garden a picture? Where does Jesus get rest and give rest? I would suggest that the garden is a picture of the church. In Psalm 132:13-16, speaking of the church, God says, 'For the Lord has chosen Zion; he has desired it for his dwelling place: "This is my resting place forever; here I will dwell, for I have desired it. I will abundantly bless her provisions; I will satisfy her poor with bread. Her priests I will clothe with salvation, and her saints will shout for joy."' Spurgeon said of this rest of God: 'A Sabbath for the Eternal and a place of abiding for the Infinite. He calls Zion *my rest*. Here his love abides and displays itself with delight.... He will not seek another place of repose, nor grow weary of his saints.'[2] The church, with all its means of grace, is the garden where Jesus and his bride share his possessions. There he feeds them from the trees that grow in the garden; there he reveals himself (in picture form he is about to liken himself to various flowers in the garden).

We saw that before the woman was taken into Solomon's palace she was outside, being forced to work in the midday sun by her natural brothers. She was in need of rest and recovery, and here her Beloved is personally giving it to her. And this is what should happen in church: we come in from our hard, dry, unsympathetic world and discover afresh the solace and restoration found in the Lord's garden, his church.

The two trees and the green grass of the garden of Solomon picture *incorruptibility*. The cedar was famous for the long-lasting nature of its wood; the fir tree is an evergreen tree; the grass was kept green by the permanent supply of water. This points to the indestructibility of Christ's church. The devil got into the Garden of Eden and succeeded in turning it into a wilderness. But he cannot

---

[2] C. H. Spurgeon (rpt. 1978), *The Treasury of David*, Evangelical Press, Vol. 4, p. 102.

do that to the church despite the many temptations and problems he causes. Here, in the garden of the church there is security while we recover from the spiritual stresses on our souls.

The king   ¹I am a rose of Sharon,
a lily of the valleys.
²As a lily among brambles,
so is my love among the young women
(Song 2:1-2).

7

Jesus Reveals Himself to His Bride

SONG OF SOLOMON 2:1-2

We noted in the previous chapter that the king and his beloved are now walking in the palace gardens. They compare themselves and one another to various plants, trees and vegetation found there.

1. The speaker

The speaker in 2:1 has been disputed, with some commentators saying that the man is speaking and others arguing that it is the woman. The grammar of the verse does not specify if it is male or female, therefore the identity of the speaker has to be decided from the context.

In favour of applying verse 1 to the woman is the argument that verse 2 is the man's response. On this argu-ment, the woman says that she is only like weak and delicate flowers, but the king replies by saying that she is like a flower among thorns.[1] This is the view of most Jewish commentators, most modern Christian Old Testament scholars, and several devotional authors such as Hudson Taylor.

---

1 George Burrows (rpt. 1958), *Commentary on the Song of Solomon*, Banner of Truth, p. 180.

In favour of applying verse 1 to the king is the claim to be the chief flower of the rich plain of Sharon.[2] It is very unlikely that the bride would make such a claim for herself, especially in the presence of the king. So it seems to me that it is appropriate to interpret the speaker in the verse as Christ and not as the humble Christian. This was the view of most of the early Church Fathers and Puritans.

2. The Saviour when the song was written

In 2:1, the king draws the attention of the bride to himself and then in 2:2 he makes an assessment of her. He first likens himself to two flowers and then compares her to one of them. In passing, we may note the similarity between the way Jesus describes himself here and the manner by which he often described himself when he became incarnate. Here, he is the Rose of Sharon and the Lily of the Valley; in the New Testament he is the Good Shepherd, the Bread of Life, and the Door. He takes everyday things and uses them to display his uniqueness.

The first flower to which Jesus likens himself is the Rose of Sharon. Sharon was a very fruitful plain on the coast of the Mediterranean Sea and was regarded as a place of great beauty and peace (Isa. 35:1-2). I don't think it is too difficult for us to see that it can be a picture of heaven.

In Sharon there were many types of beautiful flowers, each attractive to the eye. But there was only one type that could be classified as the rose, and it was regarded as the most attractive flower of them all. In describing himself in this way, Jesus was saying that he was the Beauty of heaven, the most attractive person who lived there.

There were beautiful objects in heaven at the time this song was written. We could think of the holy angels, of Michael, Gabriel and the others. They are fair and glorious, but not as beautiful as the Son of God. We could think of the departed saints such as Abraham, Isaac and Jacob, Moses

---

2 Alexander Moody Stuart (1857), pp. 195-96.

and Aaron, the great number of the souls of just men made perfect. They are fair, being now perfect in holiness, but not as fair as the Son of God. In what ways was he fair? He was fair in his divine attributes (his character), his accomplishments (for example, his creation of the universe) and in his divine purposes (his control of providence).

We can also note several features of the other flower that is mentioned, the lily of the valleys. The lily was a white flower, and speaks of purity, and when applied to the Son of God it could refer to his holiness. This is what Isaiah saw in the vision recorded in Isaiah 6, an unveiling of the holiness of the Son of God in heaven before he became incarnate.

An unusual feature of the lily is that it bows its head, which points to humility. As we reflect on the Son of God at the time this song was written, it may be that here is being described a surprising wonder. The holiness of the Son of God in heaven is a wonder, but it is not one that surprises us; it is what we would expect. But his humility in heaven is a wonderful surprise, yet it is true. Paul says of Jesus in Philippians 2:6-7: 'Who, being in the form of God, thought it not robbery to be equal with God: but made himself of no reputation, and took upon him the form of a servant, and was made in the likeness of men.' The incarnation was an expression, perhaps the expression, of his eternal attitude of humility.

What is humility? I think it can be expressed in the desire to serve others. Humility in a believer is not a self-demeaning attitude that refuses to recognise one's gifts and abilities. It is not humility for a person whom God has gifted to refuse to use his gift; the word for that is disobedience. Humility is seen in using the gift in total dependence on God and for the benefit of others.

In heaven the Son of God, the glory of Paradise, was already functioning as the servant of God. He had taken this role in the eternal covenant and was looking forward to coming to deliver his bride.

3. The Saviour as we sing the song

Secondly, we can consider the description in the light of the incarnation, life, death, resurrection, and exaltation of the Son of God. The obvious difference in his person between the time the Song was written and today as we read the Song is that Jesus has assumed a human nature into permanent union with his divine Person. But the addition of his human nature has not diminished his beauty or defiled his humility.

Jesus, the God-man, is still the Rose of Sharon, the object of admiration and wonder. The range of his beauty has been extended by his accomplishments as the Mediator, and the hosts of heaven admire the evidences of his triumphs. Is this not the picture that is given in Revelation 5 and 6 regarding the fact that Jesus retains his wounds in his glorified state? A slain lamb is a grotesque sight, but the Lamb that was slain is a beautiful sight. Among all the heroes who inhabit the world of glory, who have attained their reward, none stands out as Jesus does in beauty.

He is also white as the lily as far as his character is concerned. Although he is now human, he still retains the awesomeness that Isaiah beheld in his vision. We can see the effect that observing the exalted Christ had on John in Revelation 1, when he fell at Jesus' feet as dead. The holiness, the distinctiveness, of Jesus is beyond our comprehension.

He is also like the lily as far as his humility is concerned. Although exalted, he is still the Father's servant. He is the prophet who teaches his church, the priest who leads the praise, and the king who rules over all things. His desire to serve is still strong, and in the future when he presents the kingdom to the Father he will still submit himself in order that God may be all in all (1 Cor. 15:28).

> Fairest of all the earth beside,
> Chiefest of all unto Thy bride,

Fullness divine in Thee I see,
Beautiful Man of Calvary!

Jesus reveals the truth about himself in order to encourage his people. The more we know of him, the more we will love him. Although we cannot see him physically, the Holy Spirit, promised by Jesus in John 16:14, takes what is his and declares it to us. The fragrance of Jesus, depicted in these flowers, is spread abroad and our souls catch something of it and pass it on to others. We see Jesus in his dignity and beauty.

4. The Saviour sings about his bride

Having described himself, Jesus now describes his bride in verse 2: 'As the lily among thorns, so is my love among the daughters.' (NKJV) He knows what she is like (a lily) and where she is (among thorns). This is Jesus' assessment of her and his expression of sympathy with her.

His assessment is that she is like himself because he compares her to a lily. In other words, he perceives her as holy and humble. Of course, her holiness is hers because his has been given to her because of her union with him. What kinds of holiness do believers possess? I would mention two: positional holiness and practical holiness.

Positional holiness occurs at conversion when each believer is set apart to God, consecrated to him. This is when they become saints. They have been purified by the blood of Jesus and cleansed from their defilement. This aspect of holiness is unchangeable. A believer cannot cease to be a saint. This permanent status possessed by his people gives great satisfaction to Christ.

The other type or aspect of holiness is practical holiness which is a progressive state of developing conformity to the likeness of Christ. Jesus prayed for this in John 17 when he said, 'Sanctify them through your truth.' The more like him we become, the greater is his delight concerning us.

Giving the gifts obtained for men,
Pouring out love beyond our ken,
Giving us spotless purity,
Bountiful Man of Calvary!

As with Jesus himself, the illustration of the lily highlights one aspect of our characters: humility. I suppose it is improper to wonder what the most desirable grace is; but if we could, no doubt love should be given that title. But what are the manifestations of Christian love? Often we mention things like sacrificial giving, dedicated obedience, and so on. But can a lover of Jesus be identified by a feature that definitely indicates he or she is a true Christian? I suspect it can be done, and that feature is humility.

Humility is the way to receive grace: 'Clothe yourselves, all of you, with humility toward one another, for "God opposes the proud but gives grace to the humble"' (1 Pet. 5:5). It is the evidence that we have the mind of Christ (Phil. 2:3f.). 'Our piety may ever be judged by our humility,' says George Burrows.[3]

This illustration also reveals Christ's sympathy for his suffering people because he knows that they live among thorns. Thorns are a graphic picture of worldly people; they can cause pain in a variety of ways to believers: distress because of their sinful living, concern for their eternal destiny, sadness and hurt because of opposition, even physical pain. Jesus knows what such sorrow is like because he experienced it himself.

Notice two things about the thorns. First, the presence of thorns is not evidence that Christ's love for us has decreased. He addresses her as 'my love' as she goes through her pain. Second, Jesus is pleased when the thorns do not defile our holiness. These things could make us sin in one way or another (impatience, rash words) or cause us to question

---

[3] George Burrows (rpt. 1958), *Commentary on the Song of Solomon*, Banner of Truth, p. 184.

what Jesus is allowing in our lives. Yet they are allowed in order to improve our holiness.

There is a challenge here to live in a holy manner, but there is also great consolation in taking to heart Christ's assessment of us. We should not only admire him, but appropriate him and his blessings for ourselves.

> Comfort of all my earthly way,
> Jesus I'll meet Thee some sweet day;
> Centre of glory Thee I'll see,
> Wonderful Man of Calvary!

She   As an apple tree among the trees of the forest,
so is my beloved among the young men.
With great delight I sat in his shadow,
and his fruit was sweet to my taste (Song 2:3).

8

Jesus, the Apple Tree

Song of Solomon 2:3

As we noticed when considering previous verses, the couple in the Song are walking together in his garden, with each comparing the other to the trees (cedar, fir and apple) and flowers (rose and lily) that they see.

The man has described the woman as being like a lily among thorns, meaning that she is marked by features not found in other women; the features of purity in general, and humility in particular. She copies his way of describing her and now contrasts him with the men of her acquaintance when she likens him to the apple tree among the trees of the wood.

In passing, we may note that it is a good method to always copy the way that Jesus does things. Today, we have made a distinction between practice and information, with people learning lots of details that do not affect their behaviour. It was different in the Jewish world, where a teacher aimed to affect a person's conduct as well as communicate intellectual ideas. We see this in Jesus' well-known invitation to his disciples to come and learn of him in Matthew 11:28-30. In addition to teaching about the kingdom of God, he wanted to make them gentle and humble, to become like their Teacher. Another example of this method is the occasion when the disciples asked Jesus to teach them to pray (Luke 11:1), which was not a request for the latest theories on the topic, but a request based on his practice of prayer which they had observed.

The emptiness of human helps

The woman mentions two benefits from the apple tree: shade and fruit. She could not get these benefits from the other sons with whom she contrasts her Beloved. These other trees, as it were, gave her no protection or provision. They depict the reality that believers eventually realise, which is that nobody in the world can give these blessings to them. There are all kinds of human solutions to these needs of the soul – politicians, religious leaders, pleasure providers – but they turn out to be broken cisterns as far as spiritual needs are concerned.

The particular tree that is mentioned here is not our apple tree, which is not prominent in Palestine, and in any case does not provide shade. It may be a reference to the citron tree, a tree with rich foliage, which is always producing fruit, so that at any time there is a mixture of new fruit and mature fruit on its branches; yet its fruit is not sweet. Or it could be a reference to orange trees. Indeed Albert Barnes thinks that the term used here may 'in early Hebrew have been a generic name for apple, quince, citron, orange etc'. Moody Stuart comments that it 'rather seems as if by this beautiful figure the Church would set forth Christ as the Fruitful Tree amongst the fruitless, combining in itself all variety of excellence, the beauty of the apple, the refreshing juices of the pomegranate and the orange, the cool shadow and the reviving fragrance of the citron.'[1]

From what things do believers need the shade of Christ? I suppose we could approach this imagery from two vantage points. First, there is the sense in which Jesus is a permanent shade from the fury of God's wrath against our sins. This took place at Calvary, but its beneficial effects are eternal in

---

1   Alexander Moody Stuart (1857), p. 204.

that all who trust in Jesus will never face the blast of God's anger against sin. Our experience in this sense can be viewed as the weariness that resulted from fruitless attempts to find salvation by our own obedience to God's law or by good works. But we discovered that there was in Christ rest for the weary soul.

Second, there is the sense in which Jesus is a temporary shade in a wide variety of circumstances. There are outward afflictions, there are Satanic temptations, there are providential barriers, there is an accusing conscience, and there are worldly problems. All these types of things are distressing and difficult for a Christian to bear. They attack his soul. The only defence that the believer has is Jesus. With regard to some of them, the believer has to take the promises that Christ is in control and apply them to these situations. With an accusing conscience, the believer has to take the work of Christ and remind himself how it deals with his sins. Whatever the source of distress, the answer is Christ.

What fruit does Christ provide? The answer is his person and work as well as his promises. Apples are sweet fruits, and everything that Jesus did is sweet to the believer's taste. They are refreshed inwardly by thinking about various features of his life and death. There is a wide range of apples on the tree which they are expected to eat and receive benefit from. Sometimes they feed on his eternal love; at other times, his humble entrance into the world. There are his gracious interactions with sinners, his words of comfort to his people. The choice is almost limitless.

We can get an insight by thinking of the needs of a weary person and suggesting what benefits they would need. A weary person is thirsty, but Jesus is the water of life. A weary person is sore, but Jesus is the ointment to apply to these wounds. A weary person is exhausted, but Jesus is the refresher of his people. A weary person may be frightened of pursuing enemies, but Jesus is their security.

Picture of faith

The attitude of the woman here is a useful picture of faith being exercised by a believer. I would suggest that the order is important in that believers need to find rest in Christ before they can feed on Christ. They need to sit down and discover afresh the rest of Jesus before they can taste his other benefits. They need to get rid of the distractions before proceeding to his attractions.

We can imagine a harassed believer being distressed by one or more of the things that we mentioned previously. He senses that he needs Jesus but cannot focus his mind on him. He needs to sit down and apply to himself appropriate promises from the Bible. As he does this, a sense of peace begins to develop.

Sometimes, the believer has been so weakened by the harassment that Jesus graciously throws, as it were, apples to the weary saint. As the Christian sits seeking rest from Jesus, he discovers that apples are falling into his lap or around him. Jesus sends to him by the Spirit specific details about himself. In this we see the compassion of Jesus.

At other times, they need to stretch out the hands of faith and choose particular pieces of fruit. Faith at times acts *intelligently*, choosing appropriate aspects of Christ to reflect on. It also acts *innovatingly* and attempts to discover new things about Jesus. Such attempts are ways to progress in the Christian life. Faith also acts *increasingly* because every apple on the tree is hers to enjoy; so faith moves on and picks as many apples as it can. And faith acts *incessantly* because there are countless apples on this tree.

Weak faith or strong faith is marked by a common attitude, which is delight in Christ. Faith can be studied under different aspects. For example, faith can be viewed as dependence on Jesus, relying upon him alone for what the soul needs. Or it can be viewed as devotion to Jesus, an ongoing attitude of submission to his permanent authority.

The reference to delight is a reminder of the joys there are in Christian experience. Years ago, Robert McCheyne complained about a certain type of religious person and sadly they are still around. His rebuke of them is found in a sermon he preached on this verse. 'Second, some people are afraid of anything like joy in religion. They have none themselves, and they do not love to see it in others. Their religion is something like the stars, very high, and very clear, but very cold. When they see tears of anxiety, or tears of joy, they cry out, Enthusiasm, enthusiasm! Well, then, to the law, and to the testimony: "I sat down under His shadow with great delight." Is this enthusiasm? Lord, evermore give us this enthusiasm! May the God of hope fill you with all joy and peace in believing! If it be really in sitting under the shadow of Christ, let there be no bounds to your joy. Oh, if God would but open your eyes, and give you simple, childlike faith, to look to Jesus, to sit under His shadow, then would songs of joy rise from all our dwellings! Rejoice in the Lord always, and again I say. Rejoice!'[2]

In concluding this chapter, I would mention one other feature of the apple tree, which was its fragrance arising from its blossom. When a person spent time in its shade, it was inevitable that when he met up with others they could smell where he had been. Similarly, others will notice when we have spent time with Jesus because we will not only be changed, but transformed into his likeness. As Paul writes of himself and others in 2 Corinthians 2:14-15: 'But thanks be to God, who in Christ always leads us in triumphal procession, and through us spreads the fragrance of the knowledge of him everywhere. For we are the aroma of Christ to God among those who are being saved and among those who are perishing.'

The obvious lesson from this illustration is that there must be a practical implementation of our knowledge of Christ. Jesus alone can give us contentment, serenity, peace and rest. It also suggests that we need to make time for this experience and turn aside from the pressures of life and linger in his presence.

---

2   Andrew A. Bonar (1843, rpt, 1977), p. 355.

She	⁴He brought me to the banqueting house, and his banner over me was love. ⁵Sustain me with raisins; refresh me with apples, for I am sick with love. ⁶His left hand is under my head, and his right hand embraces me!
The king	⁷I adjure you, O daughters of Jerusalem, by the gazelles or the does of the field, that you not stir up or awaken love until it pleases (Song 2:4-7).

9

Jesus, Lover of My Soul

SONG OF SOLOMON 2:4-7

We have noticed that the king and his beloved have been walking in his garden and using the flowers and the trees there as illustrations of themselves. The situation now moves into a building; it is translated here as 'banqueting house', although literally it means 'house of wine'. The king has taken her into this new location.

Progression in love (v. 4)
This action of the king follows on from what she had done in the previous verse. There she had positioned herself under the apple tree, which we suggested was a picture of Jesus providing shelter, food and fragrance for his disciple. His response is to take her to another of his properties in order to give her more of his resources. The response of the king here is a picture of the response of Jesus to any of his people who show delight in him.

As we know, Jesus taught his disciples in the Upper Room that there would be a response by him to the love of his disciples. His teaching is found in John 14:21-23: "'Whoever has my commandments and keeps them, he it is who loves me. And he who loves me will be loved by my Father, and I will love him and manifest myself to him." Judas (not

Iscariot) said to him, "Lord, how is it that you will manifest yourself to us, and not to the world?" Jesus answered him, "If anyone loves me, he will keep my word, and my Father will love him, and we will come to him and make our home with him."'

Another example of this divine response is found in Revelation 3:20: 'Behold, I stand at the door and knock. If anyone hears my voice and opens the door, I will come in to him and eat with him, and he with me.' We are used to these words being used in an evangelistic sense when preaching the gospel to the unconverted, but they are initially an invitation or promise from Jesus to a believer who responds to him personally, even if he or she belongs to a backsliding congregation, as Laodicea was.

The situation described in the Song includes a reference to a banner that was displayed. It was the practice in the ancient world for kings and noblemen to put banners on their walls of their banqueting halls, announcing things that were important to them. These banners could indicate personal details or record great victories. As the woman sits in the banqueting hall, she looks at the king's banners and discovers that there is only one announcement: he loves her. Applying this to Jesus, we know that many things of great importance could be written on the banners in his banqueting hall. But all he wants recorded is that he loves his people. The great king, Jesus the Son of God, is not ashamed to erect a banner that says he is in love with sinners and intends to express his love for them.

Important banners also guaranteed *protection*. When a king erected his standard in a location, it was the equivalent of announcing that all his resources were at hand to defend that area. Similarly, this banner is an indication that Jesus will protect his people from enemy attack. The devil sees Christ's estimation of his people and determines to prevent them from enjoying this assurance of Christ's love and will instigate various attempts to harass or overpower them.

As we read this section of the poem, we discover that the woman encounters a difficulty, but not from an outside source. She had been weak from the heat of the sun previously (opposition) and found refreshment in the shade of the apple tree (Jesus). But now she has another kind of weakness, she is sick of love.

Problem with love (v. 5)

Her words do not mean that she despises what she is receiving, but that she is overcome by it. Her lover's expressions of love have caused her to faint. She looks round the banqueting hall and sees all the expressions of his love. The table is piled high with enticing dishes (God and his ways), the guards (the angels) are on duty, she senses the joy and happiness of the place, and the king himself is there. If she is going to enjoy more of all this provision, she needs to be strengthened.

I suppose the experience and marvel of the Queen of Sheba when she observed the riches of Solomon gives us an insight into what the woman in the poem would feel. 'And when the queen of Sheba had seen the wisdom of Solomon, the house that he had built, the food of his table, the seating of his officials, and the attendance of his servants, and their clothing, his cupbearers, and their clothing, and his burnt offerings that he offered at the house of the LORD, there was no more breath in her' (2 Chron. 9:3-4). It is similar with regard to a believer's relationship to Jesus.

John Bunyan, in his *Pilgrim's Progress*, alludes to this passage from the Song. He describes Christian and Hopeful walking through the land of Beulah: 'Now, as they walked in this land, they had more rejoicing than in parts more remote from the kingdom to which they were bound; and drawing near to the city, they had yet a more perfect view thereof: It was builded of pearls and precious stones, also the streets thereof were paved with gold; so that, by reason of the natural glory of the city, and the reflection of the sunbeams upon it, Christian with desire fell sick; Hopeful also had a fit or two of the same disease: wherefore here they lay by it a while, crying out because of their pangs, "If you see my Beloved, tell him that I am sick of love."'[1]

In the last sickness of John Welch, the Scottish Reformer and son-in-law of John Knox, he was overheard to say, 'Lord, hold thy hand, it is enough; thy servant is a clay vessel, and can hold no more.'[2] Expressions of divine love can be very over-powering for our weak frames.

We can think of Paul's words in his prayer recorded in Ephesians 3, which is a prayer of intercession that his readers would know the love of Christ experimentally. He describes the experience in this way: 'so that Christ may dwell in your hearts through faith – that you, being rooted and grounded in love, may have strength to comprehend with all the saints what is the breadth and length and height and depth, and to know the love of Christ that surpasses knowledge, that you may be filled with all the fullness of God' (3:17-19). This is a wonderful experience. Note, however, that Paul knows that these believers cannot experience it until they have been 'strengthened with power through his Spirit in your inner being' (3:16).

Aware of her weakness, she asks for help. But she does not ask for help from her Beloved. The objects of her request to 'Stay me with flagons, comfort me with apples' are plural, so it is a request to her companions, the daughters of Jerusalem, her fellow believers. The plural request indicates that the king and his lover are not in a private location, but in a place where her attendants are also present. Applying this to Christ and his people suggests that this incident does not picture a Christian having rich fellowship with Christ by himself or herself, rather it points to an occasion of corporate fellowship such as church services or meetings for fellowship and mutual discussion.

---

1   John Bunyan (1895, rpt. 1997), *The Pilgrim's Progress*, Banner of Truth, p. 179.

2   James Young (1866), *Life of John Welch*, John Maclaren, p. 405.

What is pictured in the items she asks for? Flagons were used for two purposes: holding wine or holding flowers. Apples were also used for producing a special fragrance. The picture is of the woman asking her attendants to take near to her the flagons and apples that were on the king's table. In a sense, it does not matter if the flagons contain wine or flowers because the point in question is do with reviving her from her weak state, as did the fragrance of the apples (there is the possibility that 'flagons' should be translated as 'raisins', and they also were used to give strength to those who were faint, 1 Sam. 30:12). The daughters of Jerusalem are to take what they can from the king's table and use it to revive the fainting woman.

Applying this to the people of God, we can picture it this way. Here is a believer meeting with God's people in a public way. During the meeting her soul feels overcome by the love of Jesus. What does she need to receive in order to be strengthened? The poem suggests that she needs to sense the fragrances from the king's table through the lives of her friends. Contrary to other situations in which a person is weakened when others take away from the available supply, the Christian is strengthened when he experiences others sharing with him what they have received from Christ's bounty.

I suppose we can apply this to the Lord's Supper. Here is a Christian enjoying in her soul fresh experiences of the love of Jesus. Her heart overflows, and it is too much to bear. As she looks round at her fellow-communicants, she senses that they have brought their personal experiences of Christ with them. One is going through difficult providences but is receiving special help from Christ, another is a new believer who is full of the joy of salvation received from Christ, and another has just enjoyed answers to prayer from Jesus. The fragrances of the king's table are blowing and they refresh her fainting soul.

I suppose we could wonder why the king himself did not carry the flagons and apples to the woman. I suspect the answer is that it was the attendants' duty to do it, that it was one of their roles to perform as they were given privileged access to the presence of the king. Similarly, believers are meant to help one another. We can think of many examples. The psalmist in Psalm 66:16 says: 'Come and hear, all you who fear God, and I will tell what he has done for my soul.' Paul writes in 2 Corinthians 1:3-4: 'Blessed be the God and Father of our Lord Jesus Christ, the Father of mercies and God of all comfort, who comforts us in all our affliction, so that we may be able to comfort those who are in any affliction, with the comfort with which we ourselves are comforted by God.' In 2 Corinthians 13:11, he writes: 'Finally, brothers, rejoice. Aim for restoration, comfort one another, agree with one another, live in peace; and the God of love and peace will be with you.' There are many other similar exhortations. The best way we can stimulate one another is by having the fragrance of the king's table.

Peace from the king (v. 6)
The fainting woman is next portrayed lying down, receiving comfort from the Beloved. He is pictured as simultaneously holding her head up and caressing her face gently. In the poem, his actions follow on from the contribution of the daughters of Jerusalem. Spiritually, this passage is telling us that our Beloved can provide more assurance than can our brothers and sisters, but that often his is given in addition to theirs.

She is resting in Christ, aware of the security of his strength and the gentleness of his touch. This is the rest of enjoyment, like that of a mountaineer who scans the view from the top of the mountain after an arduous climb. This is the rest of attainment, of sensing in a unique and wonderful way that Christ loves me, cares for me, and delights in me.

The King's Admonition (v. 7)
This is followed by the king addressing the daughters of Jerusalem and warning them not to disturb her rest. He refers

to sensitive animals that will run away at the slightest noise as pictures of how easily the rest of his lover can be destroyed. Her companions are not to make any adverse sounds. This tells us that we have to be very careful about disturbing the rest that another believer is receiving from Jesus. Even a small wrong action by another believer can remove that sense of rest. These actions could involve worldly matters, harsh words, and inappropriate comments. They grieve the Spirit of Christ who is indwelling the listener. Paul says in Ephesians 4:29-30: 'Let no corrupting talk come out of your mouths, but only such as is good for building up, as fits the occasion, that it may give grace to those who hear. And do not grieve the Holy Spirit of God, by whom you were sealed for the day of redemption.' We should always wonder if another believer is enjoying rest in Christ and ask ourselves if what we are about to do or say will affect it. After all, Jesus does not want their rest disturbed.

Poem 3

Summer in the Soul (2:8-17)

She   ⁸The voice of my beloved!
Behold, he comes,
leaping over the mountains,
bounding over the hills.
⁹My beloved is like a gazelle
or a young stag.
Behold, there he stands behind our wall,
gazing through the windows,
looking through the lattice.
¹⁰My beloved speaks and says to me:
'Arise, my love, my beautiful one, and come away,
¹¹for behold, the winter is past;
the rain is over and gone.
¹²The flowers appear on the earth,
the time of singing has come,
and the voice of the turtledove is heard in our land.
¹³The fig tree ripens its figs,
and the vines are in blossom;
they give forth fragrance.
Arise, my love, my beautiful one,
and come away' (Song 2:8-13).

10

The King's Invitation

SONG OF SOLOMON 2:8-13

Verse 8 begins a new poem that runs down to the end of chapter 2. The poem begins with a reference to mountains that the king has to cross and closes with a reference to the mountains of Bether (meaning separation), so there is a kind of inclusio. As with the previous poem, there are three speakers: the king, his beloved and her assistants. The woman describes the approach of the king in verses 8 and 9, she records his appeal in verses 10-13, she reveals this desire for her in verse 14, she mentions the joint request of herself and the daughters of Jerusalem in verse 15, and the woman speaks in verses 16 and 17.[1]

In this poem, the woman is described as being in two places. First, she is located inside a walled house where she has been for the winter, but now the summer has arrived and the king comes and calls to her. Second, she is likened

---

1 Regarding this particular poem in the Song, Robert Murray McCheyne said, 'We might well challenge the whole world of genius to produce in any language a poem such as this – so short, so comprehensive, so delicately beautiful. But what is far more to our present purpose, there is no part of the Bible which opens up more beautifully some of the innermost experience of the believer's heart' (Andrew A. Bonar [1844, rpt. 1892, 1978], p. 482.).

to a dove taking refuge in rocks, and again the king comes and speaks to her. In the structure of the poem, the woman becomes like the dove in the rocks because of the effects of the king drawing near to her in the walled house.

The approach of the king (v. 8)

The king is likened to a deer skipping over mountains. These mountains and hills are the barriers he has to cross before he can draw near. In the poem, the woman can hear his voice as he crosses these barriers. She speaks from the perspective of one who already has had a relationship of love to him because she calls him, 'my beloved.' She has learned to recognise his voice because he has been with her before.

This description of barriers points to the common Christian experience of our sins having raised a barrier between us and Christ. We caused the barrier even although we had experienced his mercy and known his love. At our conversion, we began to know that love which had no beginning. We discovered that he had loved us with an everlasting love, a love which he had expressed for us in the eternal counsels. We also discovered that he loved us with a sacrificial love, that he had freely and gladly taken our place on the cross and borne God's wrath against our sins. His love was also a searching love as he sought us as the Good Shepherd and placed us on his shoulders, rejoicing when he found us. When we tasted this love for the first time, we thought our delight in it would never be hindered or lowered. It is true that some Christians manage to attain to an ongoing enjoyment of this love; I suppose the apostle John was one such person. But most Christians sadly lose their first love.

When this happens, they experience winter in their souls. What are some of the signs of winter? There is coldness and fruitlessness. This was the case with the bride here. She had shown coldness to the king and he had withdrawn himself. She was still living in one of his houses, but his presence was not known by her. Is this not a picture of times when believers come to church and sense Christ is not there because they are enduring winter in their souls?

It seems to me that the woman is looking out for the king to come and get her. Therefore, she hears his voice from a distance before she hears him speak closely outside the door of the house. Because she has heard him in the distance, she anticipates meeting with him when he comes to the house in which she is living. Is there an equivalent to this in the Christian life? I would suggest that the counterpart to the king's voice being heard at a distance is the promises in the Bible. The promises come for a wide variety of circumstances, including restoration from a barren period in a believer's life. These promises encourage the believer as he senses the winter in his soul.

Eventually the king reaches the house in which she is living, which I think is a picture of the church. I suppose we could say that the church in Laodicea was experiencing winter when Jesus came knocking at the door.

Before we consider the way Jesus displays himself in the church, we should note that the image of an agile deer leaping across the mountains suggests the speed with which Jesus can fulfil the expectation created by his promises.

The activities of the king (v. 9)

In the poem, the woman describes three activities of the king: he looks over the wall, he looks in the windows, and he reveals himself through the lattice. The point is that he places himself at the locations where she can see him. What are the locations within the church where Jesus can be seen? The answer to this question is the means of grace: these include the singing of psalms, the reading of the Scriptures, the preaching of the Word, and the celebration of the Lord's Supper. In each of them, Jesus tells us something about himself.

It is important that we see these various means in this light. The singing of the psalms is a means by which Jesus meets with us. A basic fact is that Jesus, when he was on earth, sang the psalms although he would apply them to himself in different ways from what we do at times. But it is a useful exercise to ask ourselves, when looking at a psalm, how does it apply to Jesus? Sometimes it is a prophecy (22, 110), sometimes it is a praise of God (imagine Jesus singing psalm 100), sometimes it is a picture of Jesus (1, 15), sometimes it is a pointer to him (51, which not only describes David's repentance but indicates the necessity of a better sacrifice than was found in the rituals of Israel).[2]

When we hear the Bible being read, Jesus is speaking to us. The eternal Word addresses us each time a verse from the Scriptures is read. This is one reason why it is authoritative. Peter says that the messages of the Old Testament prophets were given to them by the Spirit of Christ who was within them (1 Pet. 1:11), and Jesus sent the Holy Spirit to guide his apostles into all the truth (John 16:13), including the truth that was to be written down in the New Testament. When we hear the Bible, we are hearing prophecy (forth telling and foretelling), and true prophecy, which the Bible is, is alive. Jesus was involved in the production of the Word, he is involved in the recitation of it, and he is involved in the proclamation of it.

Preaching is not merely a man giving his opinions of a passage; rather it is the Prophet of the church, who is Jesus, using the preacher to instruct and feed his people. Our forefathers regarded the sermon as the most important part of the service because in the other parts we speak to Christ (praise, prayer) but in the sermon he speaks to us. The Larger Catechism Question 155 asks: 'How is the Word made effectual to salvation?' Its answer states: 'The Spirit of God maketh the reading, but especially the preaching of the

---

[2] A very useful book explaining the use of the psalms in worship services is Michael Lefebvre (2010), *Singing the Songs of Jesus*, Christian Focus Publications.

The King's Invitation

Word, an effectual means of enlightening, convincing, and humbling sinners; of driving them out of themselves, and drawing them unto Christ; of conforming them to his image, and subduing them to his will; of strengthening them against temptations and corruptions; of building them up in grace, and establishing their hearts in holiness and comfort through faith unto salvation.' This is not to say that a minister's address cannot be questioned; he can make mistakes. The wonder is that Jesus uses a fallible man to communicate with his people about himself. Of course, these fallible men are guided by the Spirit, usually secretly but sometimes consciously.

The Lord's Supper is a means by which Jesus meets with his people. As we know, there are different understandings of the Lord's Supper found in evangelical churches. Some make it only a remembrance meeting; often they will call the service by the biblical title 'breaking of bread'. Others make it a thanksgiving and they call the ordinance by the title 'Eucharist'. Both these meanings are true, but they are not sufficient. Our heritage calls it 'communion', not primarily because we have fellowship with one another but because we have communion with the risen Christ through the Holy Spirit. Jesus reveals himself to our souls as we recall with gratitude his holy life, his past sacrifice, his current intercession and reign, and his future return.

What is a church meeting? It is a gathering of those who have heard the voice of Christ in his promises and have come together in the hope that he will draw nearer to their souls.

The appeal of the king (vv. 10-13)

The woman has gone through a winter experience. I earlier mentioned the reality of the sins of a believer becoming a barrier between him and Jesus. There are other possible causes of winter in our souls. One such is testing providences when dark nights are on our soul and we long for the coming of the warm days. We cannot understand these providences and our minds are full of questions. In such situations, we also hear the voice of Jesus at a distance. At times, these winter occasions can become darker because Jesus seems to withdraw his presence, we do not sense his warmth in our souls, and cannot even hear his promises. Yet eventually Jesus draws near.

Notice the first words of Jesus to his lover who has had a winter experience, be it one of sins regretted or one of puzzling providences. He says to her, 'My love, my fair one.' Recall the various greetings that Jesus gave to his disciples after his resurrection despite their unbelief regarding it; these greetings were marked by encouragement and forgiveness. Their winter experience has not resulted in his ceasing to love them, nor has it caused him not to desire their company or to not appreciate their beauty.

If the winter was caused by the sins of the believers, then part of their fairness in his eyes will be their repentance. Repentance is an amazing grace because it gives opportunity for other graces of the soul to flourish. It deepens affection for Christ, it increases admiration of Christ, and it stimulates allegiance to Christ.

If the winter experience was caused by difficult providences, then part of their beauty in his eyes is their ongoing faith in him. Puzzlement did not result in their abandoning him; indeed, like Job, they affirmed, 'Though he slay me, yet I will trust him' (Job 13:15, KJV). In an unusual way, their troubles had strengthened assurance: 'When he has tried me, I will come forth as gold,' marked by beauty (Job 23:10).

Then note the promise of Jesus to his lover who has had a winter experience. Instead of winter in the soul, there will be summer with all its beauty, joy and fragrance. Above all, there will be a fresh experience of his company.

God gives great promises to the restored backslider. One such example is his promise in Hosea 14:4-7: 'I will heal their apostasy; I will love them freely, for my anger has turned from them. I will be like the dew to Israel; he shall blossom like the lily; he shall take root like the trees of Lebanon; his shoots shall spread out; his beauty shall be like the olive, and his fragrance like Lebanon. They shall return and dwell beneath my shadow; they shall flourish like the grain; they shall blossom like the vine; their fame shall be like the wine of Lebanon.' That list of promises is similar to the language of the Song: restoration, refreshment (dew), humility (lily), strength (cedar), and fragrance. Summertime arrives in the soul of the backslider. This is great encouragement for us to return to the Lord.

God gives great comfort to his troubled people. Says the psalmist in Psalm 31:22: 'I had said in my alarm, "I am cut off from your sight."' But he was not. Through his time of trouble he prayed, and eventually he received a marvellous display of divine grace. He mentions his prayer in verse 22: 'But you heard the voice of my pleas for mercy, when I cried to you for help,' and he summarises the consequence in verse 21: 'Blessed be the Lord, for he has wondrously shown his steadfast love to me when I was in a besieged city.'

So we have seen the approach, the appearance and the appeal of the king. In the next chapter, we will observe the continued appeal of the King and the response of his lover, the Christian.

The king	¹⁴O my dove, in the clefts of the rock, in the crannies of the cliff, let me see your face, let me hear your voice, for your voice is sweet, and your face is lovely.
Daughters	¹⁵Catch the foxes for us, the little foxes that spoil the vineyards, for our vineyards are in blossom.'
She	¹⁶My beloved is mine, and I am his; he grazes among the lilies. ¹⁷Until the day breathes and the shadows flee, turn, my beloved, be like a gazelle or a young stag on cleft mountains (Song 2:14-17).

11

The King's Invitation Answered

Song of Solomon 2:14-17

These verses continue the king's invitation to his beloved to come away with him and enjoy the blessings of the coming summer. In the poem he has been away for the winter from the house where she lives, which is probably one of his palaces. She has been looking for him to come, and was aware of his voice calling out to her as he drew near the house.

As we suggested in the previous study, winter pictures the period of Christ's absence from the soul of a believer; the absence may have been caused by the believer's own sin or by the Saviour withdrawing himself in order to test his disciple. Yet throughout this winter period she has been enjoying the provision of his house (which is a picture of the church and the various means of grace that he provides there). She has been longing for his return, reminding herself of his promises. Now he has come, and in verse 14 he is continuing his appeal that he began in verse 10.

In this section of the poem, although it is the woman who speaks throughout it, she also quotes comments from the King and from the daughters of Jerusalem. As in previous parts of the Song, the daughters of Jerusalem are present with the bride, which is a picture of other believers maintaining fellowship with a believer going through a winter experience.

The request of the king (v. 14)

The king addresses her with a name that he has already used of her when he calls her 'my dove' (1:15). We noticed, when considering that previous reference, several characteristics of a dove-like person: mourning for sin (a dove gives sad sounds), marked by purity (a dove is white), desire for peace, able to see where these blessings are located – in Jesus (a dove is clear-sighted, and she has been looking at him as he leaped over the hills), and a sense of defencelessness. Although she has gone through a winter experience, his estimation of her has not changed because she is always his love. He sees her penitence, he is aware of her desire for purity, he desires to fulfil her longing for peace from him, and he is resolved to protect her at all times. If we respond correctly to a winter experience, whether caused by personal sin or adverse providences, Jesus will see in us these God-given features depicted in a dove.

The king then mentions her location: she is in the clefts of a rock, in the secret places of the stairs (or a series of rocks that looks like a staircase). Doves in that part of the world often made their nests in holes in rocks or cliffs. These rocks and cliffs were barren places and are good pictures of the winter experiences of Christians.

Jesus warned his disciples that 'In the world you will have tribulation. But take heart; I have overcome the world' (John 16:33). Although she has been in his house with all its benefits she has also been going through a winter experience that is similar to a barren location. The two experiences of desiring to meet with Christ and yet sensing his absence during a time of difficulty are not incompatible; we need only remind ourselves of Job's strong desire when he was in trouble: 'Oh, that I knew where I might find him, that I might come even to his seat! I would lay my case before him and fill my mouth with arguments' (Job 23:3-4). Yet her tough spiritual experience had helped to develop dove-like features that attracted her Beloved.

He therefore appeals to her to come out of these desert places and show her beauty to him. His voice is one of encouragement because he knows that her experiences, whether caused by personal sin or difficult providences, have made her think that she has lost her beauty. Although she was delighted when she heard his voice as he raced rapidly to the house, now that he has come near she feels unworthy to be seen by him. Her experiences have given her the grace of humility, whether it was penitence for her sin or patience in times of trouble. Humility and difficult experiences should go together in a Christian's outlook; note how Paul summarised his ministry in Acts 20:19: 'serving the Lord with all humility and with tears and with trials that happened to me through the plots of the Jews.'

Winter experiences have not only developed her beauty, they have also taught her how to speak *to* her Beloved and to speak *about* her Beloved. Therefore, he desires to hear her voice. This is the usual Christian experience. How beautifully Peter was able to speak after his restoration from his winter time of denial: his words strengthened his fellow Christians (Luke 22:32). Job, too, spoke differently after his restoration (Job 42). Many, if not most, of the psalms were beautiful words sung after times of trouble.

This desire of Jesus tells us how greatly he longs to have fellowship with each of his people. Each Christian has a unique encounter with him; unique not only because of who Jesus is, but also unique because of the particular way each Christian has been brought through his or her winter experiences into the summer time of mutual enjoyment with Jesus.

The concern of the daughters (v. 15)

The appeal of the king in this poem is not answered immediately by the woman but by the daughters of Jerusalem (notice the plural pronouns), who cry, 'Catch the foxes for us, the little foxes that spoil the vineyards, for our vineyards are in blossom.' The poem refers to the common situation in Palestine of foxes and jackals eating grapes. It was very difficult to keep them out of vineyards because they were able to burrow below the protective hedges around them. Therefore, they are a good representation of anything that destroys fruit in a believer's life. Here the song describes little foxes, which points to the destructive effects of little sins. But they need not only represent sins; they can also depict anything that hinders fruit bearing, such as periods of trouble. The daughters of Jerusalem, too, have had the winter experience of the king being absent from his house.

These companions of the bride have watched the king drawing near and have heard his loving entreaties to her. The positioning of their request before her response suggests the concerns that other believers should have about their lack of fruit hindering fellowship between Jesus and another disciple. The king is drawing near to the house they and she share. Before the king comes in to express his love in a deeper way, they ask him to deal with their failure to develop as they should have done.

This desire is evidence of brotherly love, of mutual concern among the people of God not to be a hindrance to one another in spiritual experiences. Applying it to ourselves, when we sense the king is drawing near we should make sure that our attitudes, words and actions do not disturb his approach. Each believer should have the same beauty of countenance and voice when the king draws near after a time of winter.

The delight of the bride (vv. 16-17)

The bride rejoices in the assurance that has become hers from listening to the king's assessment of her. She realises that she possesses infinite riches, Christ himself. 'He is mine by the free gift of himself to me; he is mine to look on, to lean upon, to dwell with; mine to bear all my burdens, mine to discharge all my debts, mine to answer all my accusers, mine to conquer all my foes; mine to deliver me from hell, mine to prepare a place for me in heaven; mine in absence, mine in presence, mine in life, mine in death, mine in the grave, mine in the judgment, and mine at the marriage supper of the Lamb.'[1]

She also discovers that she has the wonderful status of belonging to him. Each Christian belongs to Jesus in several

---

1 Alexander Moody Stuart (1857), p. 265.

ways. One way is by *gift* when the Father gave each of them to Jesus in the eternal counsels before the creation of the universe. They are also his by *price* because he paid the penalty of their sins when he redeemed them by his death on the cross. A third way by which they belong to him is by *conquest* because he overcame, by his gospel of grace, their opposition to being rescued by him from the state of sin and condemnation. A fourth way by which they are his is that of *relationship*, of actual union; this is depicted in the Bible by several illustrations. This union is a developing one (he is the foundation and they are the building), is a living one (he is the head, they are the body), and is an intimate one (he is the bridegroom, they are the bride).[2]

It may be the case that verse 16 is also spoken by the bride as she observes what has happened to the concerned

---

2   'And I am his. – I am his, by him created ; I am his, by him redeemed; I am twice his, by original right, and by purchase when I was lost. I am his by the ransom of his blood, his by the conquest of his Spirit, his by my own free consent; his in body, in soul, in estate; his entirely, his exclusively, his irrevocably. I am his and he will defend me, his and he will correct me, his and he will make use of me; but his and he will love me, his and he will delight in me, his and he will claim me against all rivals and opponents; yea rather, his and he doth love me, his and he doth delight in me, his and he claimeth me now against all adversaries. I am not my own, not the Church's, not the world's, not man's, not the law's, not Satan's; but his, Christ's, my Beloved's. I am not the property of time, nor of care, nor of business, nor of necessity; but of Christ, for I am his. All things, O believer! are thine in Christ; yet thou art no one's but his. All things pertain to thee; but thou pertainest to none but Jesus. Thou art the property of no man, the property of no creature, the property of no uncreated, yet mighty reality, like sin. I am my Beloved's, and none else possesses either right or power over me, except according to his will and sufferance; and if I am my Beloved's and he is mine, then all that is mine is his – all my sin, my weakness, my condemnation, and my misery; and all that is his is mine – all his strength, his righteousness, his wisdom, his holiness, his salvation, his glory. His God is my God, his Father my Father, his brethren my brethren, his heaven my home' (Alexander Moody Stuart [1857], *The Song of Songs*, James Nisbet, pp. 265-66).

daughters of Jerusalem once the king has come into the house and its garden. She says, 'My beloved is mine, and I am his; he grazes among the lilies.' The picture is of the hind, which had been leaping across the hills, coming into the garden and eating lilies there. The hind is the king and the lilies would be the daughters of Jerusalem. They were concerned that they were fruitless, but they are now enjoying his fellowship; in reality they are lilies, marked by the beauty of humility (the drooping head of the lily) and purity (the whiteness of the lily). As she observes the king and her companions having fellowship together she discovers that her sense of her own personal relationship to the King is strengthened.

The confidence with which the bride here speaks raises for us the issue of assurance. As we noticed in a previous study, the doctrine of assurance has often been likened to a three-legged chair, with each leg representing a means of obtaining assurance. The first leg is the assurance a believer obtains from biblical statements (if you trust in Christ, you will be saved); the second leg is the assurance a believer deducts from changes in his own life (hatred of sin, desires after holiness); the third leg is the assurance that is known through experiencing Christ in the inner life (witness of the Spirit, Jesus and the Father making their home in an obedient believer's heart). The first two means of assurance need to be in place before the third will function properly. The first means is external whereas the other two means are internal. It is also possible to balance the stool on the first two types (biblical statements and self-examination), but that balance is not as comfortable as what is known when the three types of assurance are working together.

It is the third type of assurance that is described here. The first leg is depicted in the voice of Jesus calling to the bride in the promises of his Word (as we noticed in the previous study), the second leg is the humility and sense of unworthiness possessed by the bride, and the third leg is the actual encounter with Jesus.

Yet the bride is aware that her current experience is not permanent. Therefore, in words that have become linked to the desire of believers for heaven, she prays in verse 17, 'Until the day break, and the shadows flee away, turn, my beloved, and be thou like a roe or a young hart upon the mountains of Bether' (KJV). It may be that this verse indicates that the king had once again left the house and she is watching him riding off towards the hills. Yet while she knows that his visit was not permanent, she also knows that he can come again; therefore she prays that he would often return to the house in the way that he has just done.

His visit has not only created desire for more visits, it has also created the longing for the experience of which these visits are foretastes. Heaven becomes more real when the King of heaven comes to us in his house (the public means of grace) and blesses us through the various means of grace experienced there. Our Christian lives should have milestones; these milestones should mark the times we have the pleasure of Christ's company, and each subsequent milestone should give us clearer sights of heaven and stronger longings for it.

POEM 4

LOOKING FOR JESUS (3:1-5)

She ¹On my bed by night
I sought him whom my soul loves;
I sought him, but found him not.
²I will rise now and go about the city,
in the streets and in the squares;
I will seek him whom my soul loves.
I sought him, but found him not.
³The watchmen found me
as they went about in the city.
'Have you seen him whom my soul loves?'
⁴Scarcely had I passed them
when I found him whom my soul loves.
I held him, and would not let him go
until I had brought him into my mother's house,
and into the chamber of her who conceived me.
⁵I adjure you, O daughters of Jerusalem,
by the gazelles or the does of the field,
that you not stir up or awaken love
until it pleases (Song 3:1-5).

12

Seeking and Finding the Beloved

Song of Solomon 3:1-5

A new poem begins here within the song and it is a short poem of five verses. Unlike previous songs there is only one speaker (the woman), although present with her are the king and the daughters of Jerusalem (v. 5). There is a similarity to the previous verses in that initially the king and the woman are separate. Yet there is also a prominent difference regarding the response to the separation: in the previous verses the king took the journey to where she was whereas in this poem it is the woman who goes looking for the king. (In passing we may note how bizarre it is to read this literally as if the bride of an earthly king would be wandering around a city at night looking for him.) This difference between the poems illustrates the variety of Christian experiences between Jesus and his people.

The pain of separation from Christ (v. 1)
In verse 1, the woman is depicted as seeking her Beloved on her bed. It is absurd to take this literally because she would know there would be no point seeking in the bedroom for someone who was absent from the bedroom. Rather this is a picture of a common Christian experience. What does it depict? The illustration of a bed does not point to spiritual

laziness. The woman is actively searching for her Beloved during these hours of darkness; she is not sleeping. Therefore we are not considering a form of backsliding. It is the case that 5:2-8, in its use of sleeping, describes the cause of the Beloved's absence to be spiritual neglect by the believer. Here, there is no hint that this is the cause.

The illustration points to personal intimacy and describes a believer looking for Jesus in the private means of grace. She has come eagerly to these means where she and Jesus have often found mutual rest, but she cannot find him there. Is this not often the case with ourselves? We turn to the Bible or to prayer, with the aim of having fellowship with Christ, but we discover that he is absent. This is a common spiritual experience in the Bible; Job and many of the psalmists often complain of having no sense of the presence of God. Yet this experience is not one to be demeaned as having no value. While this condition is not the exhilaration that can accompany precious moments of fellowship with Christ, it is a very strong evidence of the possession of spiritual life. The next best experience to having fellowship with Christ is to hunger and thirst after it.

This means that love to Christ is not dependant on a conscious meeting with him every time we engage in personal devotions. It is possible to have strong love for Christ without a sense of his sweetness in the heart. Nor does it mean that this sense of absence indicates the believer does not know what to do about her state.

The process of seeking Christ (vv. 2-3)
What did the woman do? She did not conclude that providence was indicating she should be content with an absent Lover. Instead she resolved to find him. And she knew where to look.

The first thing that she did in the poem was to go to the city. A city is made up of people and I think here it is a picture of the church. The believer who cannot sense the presence of Christ in the personal means of grace should resolve to have fellowship with the people of God because Jesus has promised to be with them. We could take the various streets and broad ways in the city to be different means of grace that are found in the church on which believers have fellowship. There are the weekly prayer meetings, the Sunday services, the Lord's Supper.

Obviously this is a sensible spiritual decision to make. Yet sometimes when we gather with God's people we cannot sense the presence of Christ. This does not mean that they are not meeting with Christ and we have to be careful, when we don't encounter him, that we do not discourage others who are. As with our spiritual temperature in private devotions, love to Christ is not removed when we do not encounter him as we engage in public fellowship with his people. The believer, who loved an absent Christ in her personal devotions, still loves the Christ who is not encountered in the public means.

In the poem, the woman persevered in her search and during it she was spotted by the watchmen of the city. Who are the watchmen? In the ancient world, watchmen were those appointed to guard the city from attack, to inform the inhabitants when someone was approaching the city, and to ensure that the citizens could move safely throughout it. It is reasonable to say that the watchmen depict the rulers of the church, the elders, that is both teaching and ruling elders.

In the poem, the woman is noticed by the watchmen. Likely there are other people on the streets, but the watchmen detect that she has a particular burden that they can help. Elders are to be on the lookout for such people, and they need to have their vision in good order. They should sense when a person is seeking their Master. Not only do they see her need, which points to their spiritual sensitivity, they are also working in harmony because she was not found by one watchman but by a group of them. Going together throughout the city enabled them to fulfil their function.

A third detail about the watchmen is that they were active in the sense that they were going up and down the city streets looking for people to help. Since they were able to point her to where the king was, I suspect Solomon expected readers/listeners to realise or imagine that the king had given the watchmen special orders to be on the lookout for her. The king has given special orders to those that rule his church to be on the lookout for those of his people who are having soul troubles and who are in need of direction towards himself.

In what ways were the watchmen able to guide the woman as she sought for her Beloved? They would have done so by repeating the directions, promises and other information given to them by the king. They would have to be ready to pass on an appropriate word of direction and encouragement. Clearly, the main way in which this is done for believers is through the regular preaching of God's Word, but it is not limited to it. The private conversation of the watchmen should also be helpful.

Preaching is not an end in itself; rather it is a bridge along which sinners go in order to meet Christ. This is obviously the case with regard to sinners being converted. Yet it is also the goal of preaching as far as believers are concerned. There are other secondary purposes such as communicating biblical details, resolving issues of conscience, detailing principles of guidance. But preaching is more than these – it is mainly a means for bringing sinners and saints into the presence of Jesus.

There are two conclusions from this picture: first, those who are seeking Jesus should seek the help of the watchmen; second, the watchmen should always be ready to point to Christ.

The pleasure of embracing Christ (vv. 4-5)

The woman says that she had to move a little beyond the watchmen before she found her Beloved. In the spiritual life, seeking believers face the danger of being satisfied with listening to good preaching or with one of the other means of grace. No doubt, preachers give words of comfort and help. They, in their role as watchmen, are near the king; it is as possible to cease searching when we are within an inch as it is possible to cease when we are a mile away from finding him.

So she pressed on in her search and found her Beloved. No doubt he drew near and revealed himself, which gave the impression that she had found him. He cannot be found until he makes himself known. This does not mean that our searching is hopeless; if we go to the public means of grace, and listen to the words of the watchmen, we will soon find him. When we seek with a loving heart, his loving heart will respond.

Holding Christ as a lover is a good picture of faith. There are many pictures of faith: leaning on Christ, trusting in Christ, following Christ etc. Embracing Christ with the arms of faith reminds us that faith is the warm clasp of love. Faith in Jesus is not a clinical arrangement. It is the meeting of two lovers, each eager to meet the other.

The woman's actions are also a picture of determination in the life of love. First, she holds him, then she will not let him go, and then she takes him to her mother's house. In public worship, she has embraced him, but she does not want the experience to end when the service is over. So she determines to take Jesus home with her (she is living in her mother's house).

Some say that the mother's house depicts the church, meaning that a believer takes Jesus with her into every activity of the church. But I think the structure of the poem, with its reference to bed, points us back to the previous reference, which we have interpreted as depicting her personal devotions. She wants to have the Jesus she embraced afresh in the public means to be with her in her personal devotions.

There is a special wonder about this taking of Christ home, into our personal devotions. This wonder is that Jesus finds rest, peace, delight, in these occasions. He rejoices to be with her during these prayer times, these meditations on the Bible, these occasions of personal praise. In her experience, the rest of heaven is known.

Yet she is aware of a danger to her new-found experience of love and, perhaps surprisingly, she does not say it is herself. Instead the danger comes from the daughters of Jerusalem, her fellow Christians. She senses that inappropriate behaviour by them could spoil her enjoyment of Christ's presence in her heart. For example, she fears that their inappropriate words could cause him, who is as sensitive as a deer that flees at the slightest noise, to flee from her. She says to them, 'Don't spoil my enjoyment of the love of Jesus. Instead help me to retain his sweetness in my soul.'

She is aware that her Beloved may rise from his rest and no doubt hopes to enjoy fellowship with him when he does. The believer who sensed the absence of Christ now senses that Jesus is enjoying being with her. She knows the experience of divine delight and contentment described in Zephaniah 3:17: 'The LORD your God is in your midst, a mighty one who will save; he will rejoice over you with gladness; he will quiet you by his love; he will exult over you with loud singing.'

Yet that is not the climax of the experience because she anticipates a time of blessing with him when he rises from his rest. But that experience remains a secret between him and her. Perhaps its absence from the poem tells us that no words, not even poetic ones, can describe it.

Poem 5

The Marriage Journey (3:6-11)

The Question:
> ⁶What is that coming up from the wilderness
> like columns of smoke,
> perfumed with myrrh and frankincense,
> with all the fragrant powders of a merchant?

The Answer:
> ⁷Behold, it is the litter of Solomon!
> Around it are sixty mighty men,
> some of the mighty men of Israel,
> ⁸all of them wearing swords and expert in war,
> each with his sword at his thigh,
> against terror by night.
> ⁹King Solomon made himself a carriage
> from the wood of Lebanon.
> ¹⁰He made its posts of silver,
> its back of gold, its seat of purple;
> its interior was inlaid with love
> by the daughters of Jerusalem.

The Exhortation:
> ¹¹Go out, O daughters of Zion,
> and look upon King Solomon,
> with the crown with which his mother crowned him
> on the day of his wedding,
> on the day of the gladness of his heart
> (Song 3:6-11).

13

Travelling Together in the City

Song of Solomon 3:6-11

These verses make up a short poem within the overall Song. The event is described from the perspective of onlookers (probably the daughters of Zion addressed in v. 11), who see a carriage or palanquin (a litter carried on men's shoulders) approaching, accompanied by an escort of soldiers. The procession would probably be led by two men holding two poles on which there would be bowls of burning fragrances. In verse 6 the onlookers ask who it is and the reply is given in verses 7-10, possibly by the watchmen, who also exhort the daughters to go and meet the procession.

As the observers look at the approaching carriage, they realise that it is Solomon, accompanied by an armed escort. Further they realise that it is a marriage carriage, therefore the reader is meant to assume that his bride is with him in the carriage (it is possible that she is in the city and he has arrived to marry her). They realise it is a marriage party because the king is wearing a crown that was given to him by his mother. The direction from which the carriage is coming is the desert. This points to their having been married in the countryside and they are now journeying together towards the city.

There is an obvious spiritual interpretation here. As we suggested in previous studies, the woman is the individual Christian. In this poem she is married to her Beloved, and is journeying with him through the desert on the way to the heavenly city. He has provided for her a carriage in which he and she will make the journey together. In this poem, their journey is being observed by those to whom they are travelling, that is, the inhabitants of the celestial city.

The location of the marriage

When did the marriage take place? The answer to this question is that it occurred at conversion. Conversion is a union of two lovers. One is the heavenly King, who has sought each of his people in love. Eventually he wins their affections and they embrace him with a warm faith.

Where did this marriage take place? It took place in the wilderness. We can imagine that a literal wedding would have taken place at a shady spot, perhaps at an oasis, where the royal tent could have been located. The conversion of a soul to Jesus takes place in the desert of this world, but the actual location of the conversion is not a barren one because there life is present in fullness. The place of each conversion is a spiritual oasis, marked by rest and refreshment and joy.

So the marriage party sets off on the journey to the city where the royal palace is located. We will join the onlookers in the city as they watch the lovers travel through the desert.

The appearance of the carriage (v. 6)

First, we should note how the carriage appears to those looking at it from the vantage point of the city. In verse 6, the carriage is said to be 'like columns of smoke, perfumed with myrrh and frankincense, with all the fragrant powders of a merchant'. Although the carriage is still some distance from the city, the fragrance of the carriage reaches the city. It has been suggested that the pillars are the smoke of the perfumes that were burned around the king and his bride, resulting in a permanent fragrance. These perfumes were the possession of the king and he gave them as a present to his bride.

It is not difficult to suggest what these perfumes are that are shared by Jesus and each of his people – they are the fragrant graces of the Spirit that he freely gives to each of his people, although he had to pay a great price to procure that Spirit for them. Each believer was a sinner with no fragrance before he or she met Jesus. Yet the strength of his fragrance became theirs, and as the onlookers see the couple drawing nearer to the city they do not sense the effects of her sin. Instead, they see the effects of his salvation, which is conformity to the image of Christ.

Of course, it is not only the onlookers or watchmen who sense the fragrance. As the heavenly couple make their way through this desert, they let those they pass smell the fragrance. The graces of the Spirit, such as love, peace, humility and the others, permeate the atmosphere in each place through which they pass in the desert.

The guardians of the people of God (vv. 7-8)

The next detail that is mentioned is *the armed guard* (vv. 7-8). In the poem they are described as experts in war, always ready for any attack from a marauding band of Arabs who often attacked wedding parties at night. The obvious lesson is that the carriage in which the king and his bride are travelling always faces the possibility of enemy assault as long as it is in the desert. Jesus and each of his people continually face this reality. Therefore it is great comfort to know that Jesus has ensured that his people will have the best defence available.

Who are the defenders of the carriage? A good suggestion is the angels, and the Bible elsewhere says that one of their functions is to serve those who are to inherit salvation (Heb. 1:14). The psalmist affirms in Psalm 34:7 that 'the angel of the Lord encamps around those who fear him, and delivers them.' These heavenly guardians protect the people of God from attack from every direction. They were not parading in front of the carriage or behind it; instead they were all around it.

The significance of the carriage (vv. 9-10)

Then the poem refers to the *carriage* and says it was mainly built by Solomon, although 'its interior was inlaid with love by the daughters of Jerusalem'. I would suggest that the carriage depicts the church, and its various features point to aspects of the church's life.

- The carriage was made of cedars of Lebanon, the wood of which was noted for its durability. Similarly the church of Christ will last throughout the whole of human history.

- Added to the carriage were pillars of silver, over which would be hung a covering to protect from the heat of the sun. This may depict the strength of the church, able to endure all opposition.

- Between the pillars there were sheets of gold, which again point to strength and security, and that in two directions. First, those inside the chariot could lean against it and, second, arrows or other weapons launched against it would not penetrate.

- The seat on which the king and his bride sat was coloured in purple, which is the colour of royalty. This could point to the wonderful fact that each believer is a son of God, a person with royal position.

It has been suggested that once the literal carriage had been completed, the young ladies of Jerusalem would have sown flowers or other emblems, including words, on to the various fabrics of the carriage. We have already suggested in previous chapters that the daughters of Jerusalem are other believers. What contribution can they make that fits in with the items sown on the fabrics? Since the carriage depicts the church, the activity of the daughters concerns the contribution of other believers in public worship. One suggestion, following on from the custom of writing words, would be the appropriate statements that believers would say in church; there could be words of praise about Jesus, words of comfort to their fellow believer or words of intercession on behalf of their fellow believer.

The exhortation to the citizens of Zion (v. 11)

Eventually, the procession reaches the city and the watchmen or the onlookers who have seen the procession arriving call on the city's inhabitants to 'Go out, O daughters of Zion, and look upon King Solomon, with the crown with which his mother crowned him on the day of his wedding, on the day of the gladness of his heart.'

The daughters of Zion are found in two places. Some of them are the believers still in this world and others of them are the believers who are now in the heavenly city. In the imagery of the poem, the ones in heaven are urged to welcome the king as he arrives at the city with one of his people. Note that they are urged to look at the king and not at her, unlike royal weddings in this world. They are to notice two things about him. The first is the crown that he is wearing and the second is the happiness he displays.

The crown was given to him by his mother. Literally in Solomon's case, Bathsheba had to prevent usurpers from taking the crown away from him and in 1 Kings 1 we see how she intervened to ensure that Solomon would have the throne of his father David, a throne that gave him complete authority over the nation. The crown that Solomon literally wore was one that indicated he had total power. Jesus, too, has a crown that indicates he has complete authority not over a nation only but over all things.

One suggestion about what is illustrated here is this: the citizens of heaven, in welcoming a believer to the heavenly city, are urged to consider once again the way King Jesus exercised his power to ensure the safe arrival there of the believer who had been with him in the carriage. This is true of every believer as each arrives in heaven. Their arrival becomes an opportunity for the heavenly inhabitants to consider again the great power of Jesus, how he is able to overcome all the enemies who try and destroy his people on the journey to the heavenly world.

The inhabitants of Zion are also asked to focus on the joy of the King as he welcomes another disciple into the heavenly city. We often anticipate the joy of the believer as he or she enters heaven. However great that joy may be, it is eclipsed by the joy of Jesus in having with him there an individual believer who has not been in heaven before. There are many joys awaiting us in the heavenly experience, and there are many kinds of joy awaiting Jesus, one of them being the individual pleasure and delight he will experience when each believer reaches home.

The joy of Jesus is a marvellous prospect for his people. In his parable of the talents, Jesus summarised the rewards for the faithful servant as entering into 'the joy of their Lord'. This may signify his individual delight in bestowing upon each of them the blessings of heaven, but it points to more than the commencement of the reward. The statement suggests that the heavenly experience will include observing and sharing the joy of Christ. His welcome of each believer into the city of God and the subsequent sharing eternally of its resources with his people is part 'of the joy that was set before him' for which he was prepared to endure the cross and despise its shame (Heb. 12:2). We can imagine something of the joy with which Jesus turns to the heavenly Father and says, 'Look, I and the children that you gave me' (Heb. 2:13). Jesus promises his people in John 16:22: 'So also you have sorrow now, but I will see you again, and your hearts will rejoice, and no one will take your joy from you.'

We may ask why the arrival at the city is still described as part of the marriage. Comparing the details of the poem with our marriages, we can say that (1) conversion is like the marriage ceremony, (2) the whole of a believer's life is like the journey to the reception, and (3) the meal at the reception is like the marriage supper of the Lamb, and (4) the subsequent life together lasts for ever.

POEM 6

THE CAPTIVATED KING (4:1–5:1)

The King ¹Behold, you are beautiful, my love,
behold, you are beautiful!
Your eyes are doves
behind your veil.
Your hair is like a flock of goats
leaping down the slopes of Gilead.
²Your teeth are like a flock of shorn ewes
that have come up from the washing,
all of which bear twins,
and not one among them has lost its young.
³Your lips are like a scarlet thread,
and your mouth is lovely.
Your cheeks are like halves of a pomegranate
behind your veil.
⁴Your neck is like the tower of David,
built in rows of stone;
on it hang a thousand shields,
all of them shields of warriors.
⁵Your two breasts are like two fawns,
twins of a gazelle,
that graze among the lilies.
⁶Until the day breathes
and the shadows flee,
I will go away to the mountain of myrrh
and the hill of frankincense.
⁷You are altogether beautiful, my love;
there is no flaw in you (Song 4:1-7).

14

Christ's Admiration of His People

SONG OF SOLOMON 4:1-7

Another poem from the Song begins in 4:1. Within the poem there are three sections, with the first section running to the end of verse 7; the second section is made up of verses 8 to 11, with the third section being 4:12–5:1. The first two sections are spoken by the king and the third section contains a dialogue between the king and the woman. As we can see from verses 1 and 7, this section of the poem begins and ends with his loving assessment of her. Verse 6, with his words of longing for the marriage day, tells us that the description of the woman in verses 1-5 concerns his assessment of her before the marriage takes place. From a spiritual point of view, this means that Jesus is depicted as portraying the beauty of his disciple before they meet together in the eternal world of glory.

The announcement of the Beloved (v. 1)
The king says to the woman, 'Behold, you are fair, my love; behold, you are fair' (4:1). This is not the first time he has made such a statement (e.g. 2:10), which reminds us of the importance of repetition by the Lord Jesus concerning the spiritual experience of each of his disciples. He repeats his assessment to us by various ways. One such way occurs when

we read these statements in the Bible; turning to them often will bring comfort to our hearts. A second way by which he repeats his words of love is through sermons when Christian preachers mention them in their addresses. And a third way by which he does it is through the Holy Spirit bringing these declarations of love to our minds and hearts. We should be on the alert for these assertions by Jesus.

Disciples should be comforted by this affirmation of the relationship that exists between Christ and his people. *Corporately* they are his love and *individually* they are so as well. Note the double use of 'behold'. The plural usage points to Christ's intense desire to inform his disciple of his estimation. Yet there is more than a desire to pass on information, important as that is. We could say that Jesus wishes to inflame our emotions as well as inform our minds. When another believer affirms their love to us, we don't respond merely by saying, 'Thank you for letting me know that you love me.' Instead we sense a bond of love between us and that believer. This should be the case between each believer and Jesus, except at a far higher level.

Jesus' assessment of each Christian includes the description that every one of them is 'fair'. What does he mean? Obviously he is making a contrast between a Christian and a non-Christian. The latter is marked by no soundness from the sole of his foot to the top of his head (Isa. 1:6). In contrast, each believer is depicted as being exceedingly fair.

The admiration of the Beloved (vv. 1-5)
The king gives a sevenfold description of the beauty of the woman. He refers to her eyes, her hair, her teeth, her lips, her temples, her neck and her bosom. Each of her features is described by an appropriate illustration. Her eyes are peaceful, her hair is thick and long, her teeth are even and white, and so on. Obviously, the description details a woman of great beauty and ideal balance.

Christ's Admiration of His People

James Durham mentions that Solomon is using the beauty of the outward person to depict the beauty of the Christian. (In passing, we can note that this is not an unusual feature from the ancient world; for example, statues of human beings were used to depict various ideals such as wisdom and love.) Durham goes on to argue that each of the details have an exact spiritual equivalent.[1] While I think his suggestion concerning the inner man is correct, I don't think it is necessary to look for particular equivalents in a disciple's spiritual form, except to say that Jesus has a similar outlook towards the spiritual beauty of his disciple as the king had towards the woman. He has chosen several striking images to illustrate her beauty.

Seven details are mentioned and this would indicate that here we have a perfect picture of a character (seven is the ideal number). In applying the imagery to a disciple, we can think of various graces that make a believer beautiful in the sight of Christ. There are several groups of graces found in the Bible, such as the Beatitudes or the fruit of the Spirit. These are the features that Jesus finds attractive.

The list of beautiful features indicates that Jesus loves to consider in detail the various graces that mark each of his people. We know that there are two ways to consider a beautiful object. One way is to look at its entirety; the other way is to look at its various details. The second practice is mentioned here. We should picture Jesus drawing near to each of his people and enjoying assessing each aspect of their Christian lives.

What beauties does each child of God permanently possess? There is the beauty of justification, the standing of forgiveness and acceptance that every believer has before God the judge. The delightful obedience of Jesus is imputed to us, his lovely life lived on behalf of sinners; the beautiful atoning death of Jesus, by which he paid the penalty for our sins, gives to us the attractiveness of forgiveness. 'But to the

---

[1] James Durham (1840, rpt. 1997), pp. 199-200.

receiving soul is given the undivided Christ, made of God wisdom, righteousness, sanctification, and redemption; and Jesus recognising his own garment of salvation declares – Thou art all fair, my love, there is no spot in thee.'[2] This is one way by which Jesus sees our beauty.

Another aspect of beauty that Jesus beholds in each of his people is the wonder of adoption into God's family. Each of them is exalted to this high status of membership of the heavenly family. Jesus, the Elder Brother, addresses each of them as brethren.

A third permanent feature of beauty that marks every believer is his or her possession of the Holy Spirit. Within each of them dwells the third Person of the Trinity, and this indwelling sets them apart to God and sanctifies them. Sanctification has its definitive as well as its progressive aspects. Every Christian is marked by the beauty of possessing permanently the gracious Holy Spirit. And Jesus sees this beautiful feature as he contemplates each of his disciples.

Thinking of this divine visit may cause us to feel apprehensive. But we should not do so, because the Lord Jesus does not draw near to condemn us or to discourage us. Instead he draws near to savour the work of divine grace in our souls. He is delighted by our love to him, our desire for him, our willingness to serve him. Further, he is aware of our sense of sinfulness and he desires to assure us that he still delights in us and desires our company.

The beauty of the woman points to the balanced way in which grace develops in a believer's life. She does not have a holy will and an unholy imagination. Rather every aspect of her character has its gracious features. She is not yet perfect, but she is not fully imperfect either. She is developing in Christlikeness, which is evidence of great beauty.

Another aspect worth considering is that the fairness or the beauty of Christians also includes their potential. This

---

2 Alexander Moody Stuart (1857), p. 325.

is hinted at in the poem when the king links the beauty of the woman to the marriage day that is yet to dawn. We can imagine a great king, on marrying a poor girl, anticipating the great changes that are going to come into her experience through his riches. She cannot imagine these changes at the time; at present she is enjoying the wonders of his grace in determining to marry her, and these marvels are sufficient to overcome her. Gradually she will experience something of his glory as she proceeds in the marriage. In a similar way, each Christian on earth is focussed on the wonders of the grace of Christ in bringing about this astonishing relationship; in heaven, in the eternal world, every Christian will further appreciate the glories of Christ and be transformed into his likeness. Although these believers cannot see their potential, Jesus does, and he affirms that each of them is fair.

The absence of the Beloved (v. 6)

The Beloved intimates that he is about to leave and go and dwell in a mountainous place which he describes as the mountain of myrrh and the hill of frankincense. Various interpretations have been given of this location.

One interpretation takes these hills to depict the place of intercession, the throne of grace which was depicted by the mercy-seat in the temple. The mercy-seat in the temple was always surrounded by the fragrance of incense. This interpretation suggests that Jesus says to his disciple, 'The place where you and I will meet until the great day comes will be the place of prayer. There we will have communion together.' The sweet aroma that permeates this meeting is the fragrance of the Spirit. That fragrance is perfect in Jesus and is developing in his disciple. Burrows, who takes this interpretation, notes the appropriateness of describing the throne of grace as a mountain – it pictures a place of elevation, a place with a purer atmosphere than the world. 'Whenever we wish to meet with Jesus, we have only to betake ourselves to the place of prayer.'[3] While it is obvious that such meetings with Jesus are important and essential, it is difficult to see how they are different from the meetings already pictured in the Song of Solomon. Verse 6 points to an activity that Jesus does by himself, without the involvement of another person.

A second interpretation is to see two mountains or hills, with the first, the mountain of myrrh, referring to Calvary and the second, the hill of frankincense, referring to heaven and his intercession. The mountain of myrrh is said to refer to Calvary because myrrh has to be crushed before its fragrance is known. This interpretation views the statement from the perspective of an Old Testament believer, with Jesus mentioning two future events that were necessary before the permanent togetherness of his people would occur.

A third interpretation, which I think is the best option, sees both hills as descriptive of the same place, heaven. With New Testament eyes we can see how heaven can be fragranced by the sweet aroma of myrrh because the air of Paradise is perfumed by the odour of the sacrifice of Jesus. Heaven enjoys the twofold effect of the fragrance of Jesus: the beautiful perfume of his divine person and the unique aroma of his sufferings. He has gone there to prepare a place for each of his people, to await their arrival. And as he goes, he reminds his disciples that the reason for his separation is not a defect in them because he sees no fault in them.

Sometimes it is interesting to observe how a biblical phrase reappears in a person's outlook. One of my favourite historical characters is Andrew Bonar. Many aspects of his life have been observed and on one occasion I was impressed by his several references to the mountains of myrrh and hill of frankincense throughout his written works. Here is a sample of them and I hope you find it helpful in a spiritual way to note how this description helped Bonar to think of heaven.

---

3   George Burrows (rpt. 1958), pp. 289-91.

Bonar is best known for his *Memoirs and Remains of McCheyne*, published after McCheyne's death. Regarding him, Bonar wrote: 'His tomb may be seen on the pathway at the north-west corner of St Peter's burying-ground. He has gone to the "mountain of myrrh and the hill of frankincense, till the day break and the shadows flee away." His work was finished. His heavenly Father had not another plant for him to water, nor another vine for him to train ; and the Saviour who so loved him was waiting to greet him with his own welcome: "Well done, good and faithful servant, enter thou into the joy of thy Lord."'[4]

Shortly after the death of McCheyne in 1843, Bonar was one of the preachers at a communion. One of his elders recorded the occasion: 'The congregation met in a large canvas tent. The day was bright and sunny. Mr. Bonar's closing address after the Tables was on Song iv.6: "Until the day break, and the shadows flee away." He referred to Mr. McCheyne as standing on the "mountain of myrrh" till the day break, and, as he pointed to the bread and wine before him as shadows that would flee away, there came a great hush over the congregation, and then the sound of sobbing from the Dundee people who were present, at the mention of their beloved minister's name. Mr. Bonar himself was much affected; indeed it was a weeping congregation.'[5]

Years later, in 1884, Bonar wrote a letter to a person who had been bereaved and in it mentioned this interpretation: 'Dear Margaret, I was greatly surprised on receiving your letter. But I suppose you were your self taken altogether unawares. This comfort, however, you have, sure and full, viz., that E. has only gone to "the mountain of myrrh and hill of frankincense" for a season, and then shall come back with Christ in immortal health, soul and body. You can think of her every day as "with Christ" in the Paradise above, enjoying

---

4   Andrew Bonar (1844, rpt. 1978), pp. 164-65.
5   Marjory Bonar (1895), *Reminiscences of Andrew A. Bonar*, Hodder and Stoughton, p. 18.

blessedness to which we here are strangers, and you may be sure that the Lord intends for you some peculiar blessing by this sore bereavement. What a word that is in Hebrews 12:10: affliction sent not only that we may get some profit by it, but "that we may be partakers of His holiness".'[6]

Seven years later, Bonar wrote to the wife who had lost her husband and again he used this interpretation to remind one of heaven: 'My Dear Mrs. Mudie, I was altogether taken by surprise when the news came, "Mr. Mudie is gone!" gone to the "mountain of myrrh and hill of frankincense *till the Daybreak*." You do not know how many of Christ's friends here and elsewhere will miss him. All of us felt, when we were privileged to have his visits, that we had among us a man of God, full of faith and of the Holy Ghost, full of brotherly love also in no ordinary degree, and bright in spirit with the hope of soon meeting his Lord. But, dear sister, shall not you and yours lift up your heads and "rejoice with them that do rejoice"; rejoice with him who today sings before the Throne: "*His presence fills each heart with joy.*" And then the Day of our Gathering together in Christ, how near it may be! Samuel Rutherford would have reminded you as he reminded a dying friend: "Ye will not sleep long in the dust before the Daybreak. It is a far shorter piece of the night to you than to Abraham and Moses." Nor will the Comforter forget to bring you many a message from our sympathising High Priest, who spoke that word at the grave of Lazarus, "If thou wilt believe, thou shalt see the glory of God", in this bereavement. We will pray for you all, that your consolation may abound.'[7]

One of Bonar's heroes was Samuel Rutherford and of him Bonar wrote, 'His description of himself on one occasion is, "A man often borne down and hungry, and waiting for the marriage supper of the Lamb." He is now gone to the

---

[6] Marjory Bonar (1895), *Reminiscences of Andrew A. Bonar*, Hodder and Stoughton, p. 235.

[7] Ibid., pp. 245-46.

"mountain of myrrh and the hill of frankincense"; and there he no doubt still wonders at the unopened, unsearchable treasures of Christ. But O for his insatiable desires Christward! for ten such men in Scotland to stand in the gap! – men who all day long find nothing but Christ to rest in, whose very sleep is a pursuing after Christ in dreams, and who intensely desire to "awake with His likeness".[8]

---

8 Andrew A. Bonar (1905), *Letters of Samuel Rutherford*, Oliphants, p. 30.

The King   ⁸Come with me from Lebanon, my bride;
come with me from Lebanon.
Depart from the peak of Amana,
from the peak of Senir and Hermon,
from the dens of lions,
from the mountains of leopards.
⁹You have captivated my heart, my sister, my bride;
you have captivated my heart with one
    glance of your eyes,
with one jewel of your necklace.
¹⁰How beautiful is your love, my sister, my bride!
How much better is your love than wine,
and the fragrance of your oils than any spice!
¹¹Your lips drip nectar, my bride;
honey and milk are under your tongue;
the fragrance of your garments is like the
    fragrance of Lebanon
(Song 4:8-11).

15

Jesus is Enthralled by His People

SONG OF SOLOMON 4:8-11

As we suggested in the previous chapter, these verses are the second section of a poem that runs from 4:1 to 5:1. In the first two sections, the king addresses the woman, whereas in the third section (4:12–5:1), they both speak. The king had detailed her beauty in the first section before leaving to go to the mountains of myrrh, which we suggested was a picture of Jesus living in heaven until the day breaks and the shadows flee.

Conversion to Jesus (v. 8)

The poem now returns to describe the communion that exists between the king and the one he loves. It opens with him asking her to leave the mountains of Lebanon (Shenir and Hermon are names of the same mountain), which were on the northern border of Israel. Being mountains, they were obviously places where a person could obtain a good view of the surrounding countryside, although the aspect of them that is stressed by the king is their danger, particularly from wild animals.

Given its location in the poem, it is likely that there is a contrast between the mountains of Lebanon and the mountain of myrrh. If the latter depicts heaven, then the former depicts the world. Where are the mountains of Lebanon? They are on the northern border of the Promised Land. Symbolically the 'mountains of Lebanon' picture the

147

combined attractiveness and danger of the world. Solomon, in the poem, draws near and urges his love to leave that perilous location and come into the safety of his domains. In a far greater way, King Jesus comes to each of his people and urges them to come into the safety of his kingdom.

I suppose we can see this invitation in two ways. One is to regard it as the Saviour desiring the believer in his unconverted state to leave the world of danger. It is the case that there are many sinful attractions in the world that we enjoy before our conversion, although we don't see them as the location of danger because we cannot, by ourselves, see that all of them are trapdoors above the tunnel that descends to hell. It is only when Jesus draws near and opens our eyes that we see that danger is all around us.

Connected to this, we could say that it is not enough for a person to contemplate the view, as it were, of spiritual blessings but failing to enter in and enjoy them. It is possible, for example, for an individual to understand Christian doctrine without enjoying its blessings, to be attracted to a Christian lifestyle without beginning to live it. To such, Jesus says, 'Come with me.'

In the parable of the sower, Jesus mentions that the devil is active, determined to take the seed of the word out of the hearts and minds of listeners by any way he can. One way he does this is by distraction, by pointing out the pleasures and enjoyments of the world. Many a person has climbed high enough to get a view of Canaan but has never crossed into it.

The other interpretation is to see the situation as depicting a backsliding Christian. Backsliding often involves living on the borders of the Promised Land, the area over which Jesus reigns as King in a particular sense (of course, Jesus reigns over all things in a general sense but it is also the case that he reigns over the church in particular). Such believers often head off in the wrong direction down the mountain further away from the safety of Christ's kingdom. If the unconverted view the glories of the Promised Land from these mountains, the backslider looks the other way and observes the attractions of the world. Any location of potential backsliding is a place of great danger and Jesus urges his disciples to keep away from them. To such, Jesus says, 'Come with me.'

Jesus is Enthralled by His People

I recall an illustration I heard many years ago. It involved an important lady who wanted to hire a coach driver. Part of the road to her house went alongside a steep cliff. Therefore she asked each applicant how close they could drive to the edge without going over. One said a yard, another said a foot. The one that was given the job said he would keep as far away from the edge as possible. This should be our attitude towards the world. Backsliding begins when we prefer to do something else than think about Christ, when we take our eyes off his kingdom.

Contemplated by Christ (vv. 9-11)

Verses 9-11 depict the way a believer, who leaves the borders of the world, appears in Christ's estimation. Obviously he is delighted with such and gives to them great insight about himself and his plans for them. For example, Jesus reveals to them that he and each of his people are related to one another in a twofold manner. The poem uses a twofold illustration of a sister and of a bride to describe the relationship: sister depicts a tie of nature and bride depicts the tie of love.

Jesus, although he is fully God, is also fully man. Although there are many details that could be mentioned of such kinship, the one I would mention first is that of fellow-feeling. Because he is a man, he understands our frame. Think of the shepherdess in the poem. She was of a different class from King Solomon. Would he understand her needs? Whether Solomon could or not, it is clear that Jesus can understand the needs of his people. 'For we do not have a high priest who is unable to sympathize with our weaknesses, but one who in every respect has been tempted as we are, yet without sin. Let us then with confidence draw near to the throne of grace, that we may receive mercy and find grace to help in time of need' (Heb. 4:15-16). He is able to sympathise with us.

Another aspect of a believer's relationship to Jesus, which appears under the use of the term 'sister', is that of belonging to the same family. Jesus is the Elder Brother and he can say to each of his people, 'You are my brother, you are my sister.'

In the poem, Solomon had taken the poor shepherdess into his royal family, a faint picture of the change of status that Jesus gives to each of his people when brought into the family of God. So Jesus draws near and reminds her that he understands her humanness and delights in her status as a member of the family of God.

The king also calls the woman, 'my bride,' which points to another aspect of the relationship between Christ and his disciples, that of intimacy and love. Jesus says to each disciple, 'You have ravished my heart.' This is an extraordinary insight into the love of Jesus for each of his people. He is enthralled by every one of them. If we observe the progression of his esteem in the previous section of the poem, we see that he begins with her eyes and then mentions other details. In this section of the poem he says that he is affected by one of her looks and by one chain on her necklace. What this image indicates is that Jesus is greatly affected by each of our graces as well as by all of them. One look of the eye of a disciple moves the heart of Jesus.

The king then says that he admires her love, saying that it is better than wine. Wine is a symbol of the highest of joys and by means of this illustration we can see that Jesus states that he truly values the love of his people. As we think of our love for Jesus, in what ways can it be enhanced? First, we love him because he redeemed us; second, we love him because he forgave us (the woman who anointed Christ loved him much because she had been forgiven much); third, we love him because he restores us when we fall (as happened to Peter in John 21); and fourth, we love him because he is preparing a home in heaven for us. Loss of our love for Jesus cannot be counterbalanced by Christian orthodoxy or activity (as the church in Ephesus, in Revelation 2:1-7, discovered). A fearful estimation is made by Paul concerning those who don't love Jesus: 'If any man love not the Lord Jesus Christ, let him be Anathema Maranatha' (1 Cor. 16:22, KJV). There are many reasons why we should love Jesus, but it staggers us to know how much it means to him.

Jesus is Enthralled by His People

Along with the affections of her heart, the king is moved by the aroma of her fragrances. This is a common feature in the Song as a whole, with reference being made several times to the fragrances of the woman. These depict the influences of the Spirit that accompany love in the heart of the believer. They are listed in Galatians 5:22-23: 'But the fruit of the Spirit is love, joy, peace, patience, kindness, goodness, faithfulness, gentleness and self-control.' Holiness is revealed in the life of one who loves Jesus.

In verse 11, the poem describes the external evidence, as it were. Her heart and her ointments would be hidden, although the effects were not. But her speech is also attractive to the king. With regard to what is being illustrated here, we would agreed with Burrows when he applies it to Jesus: 'Here he would encourage us in communion with him by assuring us how pleasant to his heart is our language of prayer and praise.'[1] Surely this is an encouragement to us to be often in personal contact with him. It is also the case that our words about him to others are precious to Jesus.

The woman's words are described as being like milk and honey. As we know, this was the description that was given of Canaan; it was the land flowing with milk and honey. Jesus says that his bride soon speaks like an inhabitant of his country, that her speech reveals that she is now a citizen of the better land. One has only to look at the penitent criminal on the cross to note the rapid change of speech that happens to those who join the Saviour's kingdom.

Even her garments are better than the best that the world can offer. Lebanon was renowned for its fragrances, whether that of the cedar, the wood of which was used for furniture, or of its other trees, some of which were sources of frankincense. She took care how she appeared in the king's sight. Obviously, it is not one's literal attire that is in view. Clothes in the Bible often illustrate good deeds, as when believers are urged to put on the new man. What a lovely fragrance is found in those in whom the fruit of the Spirit abounds!

---

1 George Burrows (1958), p. 302.

The king ¹²A garden locked is my sister, my bride,
a spring locked, a fountain sealed.
¹³Your shoots are an orchard of pomegranates
with all choicest fruits,
henna with nard,
¹⁴nard and saffron, calamus and cinnamon,
with all trees of frankincense,
myrrh and aloes,
with all choice spices –
¹⁵a garden fountain, a well of living water,
and flowing streams from Lebanon.

She ¹⁶Awake, O north wind, and come, O south wind!
Blow upon my garden, let its spices flow.
¹Let my beloved come to his garden,
and eat its choicest fruits (Song 4:12–5:1).

16

The Walled Garden

Song of Solomon 4:12–5:1

These verses are the third section of a poem that began in 4:1. It brings in the new idea of a garden but retains ideas mentioned in the previous two sections such as the woman being addressed as a bride and a sister as well as the references to Lebanon.

The believer likened to a garden (vv. 12-15)
In these verses, the king, after re-affirming his relationship to his love, likens her to a walled garden in which there is good source of water, resulting in the ample growth of a variety of trees and spices. The imagery of a garden is a picture of a Christian disciple and this is not the only occasion in the Bible when a believer or believers are likened to a watered garden. In Isaiah 58:11, this promise is given: 'And the Lord will guide you continually and satisfy your desire in scorched places and make your bones strong; and you shall be like a watered garden, like a spring of water, whose waters do not fail.' And in Jeremiah 31:12, this prediction is made: 'They shall come and sing aloud on the height of Zion, and they shall be radiant over the goodness of the Lord, over the grain, the wine, and the oil, and over the young of the flock and the herd; their life shall be like a watered garden, and they shall languish no more.'

Before we consider the several spiritual realities to which this illustration points, we may notice that it reveals the great change that has occurred in a believer's soul. Prior to conversion, that soul was not a garden full of pleasant plants but a wilderness full of deadly weeds. This great change was brought about when the garden of the soul was bought by a new owner who, having bought it, proceeded to change it. Each believer can say, 'Jesus bought my soul by the price of his blood.'

First, the walled garden illustrates the *security* of the disciple. A wall would be erected to keep out animals that would destroy the plants, and some dangerous animals have already been mentioned in this poem. Each Christian has an enemy that is attempting to destroy him, and that enemy is the devil and his allies, the world and the flesh. Yet despite the strength of these enemies, each believer is secure. Many Bible verses indicate this. For example, in John 10:27-29, Jesus mentions the double security of each believer: 'My sheep hear my voice, and I know them, and they follow me. I give them eternal life, and they will never perish, and no one will snatch them out of my hand. My Father, who has given them to me, is greater than all, and no one is able to snatch them out of the Father's hand.' Another passage that provides a double sense of security is Colossians 3:3: 'For you have died, and your life is hidden with Christ in God.' This does not mean that the believer is not apprehensive at times. Yet even at the times when the enemies seem to be winning, they are not.

The walled garden also illustrates the *secrecy* of the disciple's experiences with Christ. A person builds walls in order to have privacy, and behind these walls, his family can meet with friends or have private events. Similarly, within the security of the believer's inner life there will be secret meetings with Jesus. The reality is that each believer has been set apart by the Lord for his enjoyment (Ps. 4:3).

A third feature of the garden was its constant *supply* of water. At first glance, this could refer to the Holy Spirit, because often water in the Bible pictures the work of the Spirit. Yet since I think the believer prays for the Spirit in verse 16, it may be that the supply of water represents something else. In Psalm 1, the water that nourishes the believer's life depicts the Word of God. Similarly, Paul writes in Ephesians 5:26: 'that he might sanctify her, having cleansed her by the washing of water with the word.' I would suggest that the water in the garden of the soul here is the Bible, with its commandments, teachings, promises and warnings. There is abundant provision in the Word of God, sufficient to deal with every situation that a believer can face.

A fourth feature of the garden is the variety of plants found within it, ranging from trees to shrubs. The soul of a believer is made up of a *range of attributes*, some mental, others emotional. They need to be continually watered by the Word of God just as the garden's vegetation needed ongoing supplies of water.

Having looked at some of the details of the garden, it is worth reminding ourselves that this is a description given by Jesus and is not a self-description by the disciple. The description is accompanied by Jesus re-affirming his relationship to his disciple (brother and lover). I think we should view this as encouraging assurance from Jesus before he comes on another visit. He draws near the soul with warm words of appreciation of her sanctification.

So here we have a picture of a believer who is secure, who has enjoyed secret meetings with Jesus, who has the Bible as a means of grace, and who has various spiritual attributes. Yet she realises that there is more to the Christian life than these blessings. She wants further visits from Jesus, and has been encouraged by Jesus to prepare for one, but before that can happen she needs the wind of heaven to blow upon her garden – she needs the Holy Spirit to refresh her and enliven her.

The believer prays for the Spirit's work and the Saviour's coming (4:16)

The woman cries to the north and south winds to come to her garden and help spread its fragrances. In her request we see a picture of a Christian disciple comparing the work of the Spirit to the two winds. Here she is not asking for conversion but for consecration. We are encouraged to pray for the Spirit's work in various passages. In Luke 11:13, Jesus teaches, 'If you then, who are evil, know how to give good gifts to your children, how much more will the heavenly Father give the Holy Spirit to those who ask him!' In Ephesians 3:17, Paul prays for his readers that Christ may dwell in their hearts by faith (which sounds like a visit from Jesus to his garden), but in order for this to happen they need to be 'strengthened with power through his Spirit in your inner being' (Eph. 3:16). If that latter passage points to the necessity of the Spirit's work in the life of a Christian, the previous passage reminds us of the availability of the Spirit for this task.

We are not to think of these winds in the manner that we experience them day by day. For us, the north wind can be a very cold wind and the south wind can be stormy. In Palestine, however, the north wind is a cooling wind and the south wind, while bringing heat, is not stormy (Job 37:17 says it is a wind that brings calm).

The believer is asking the Holy Spirit to come in ways similar to these natural winds. I would suggest that the north wind points to an essential feature of the work of the Spirit. Because it is a cool wind, it has brought to mind, for many commentators, the Spirit's ministry in conviction of sin. This may be the case here, although there is no hint of backsliding – the garden is quite healthy. It is not necessary to think that the believer here is being portrayed as backsliding. The imagery suggests otherwise, for the garden is bearing fruit. We know what it is like on a very calm day without any wind. If we walk past a garden we may not smell the aroma of the flowers. In order for that to happen, there has to be a gentle breeze blowing. I would suggest that the north wind depicts clarity. The north wind cleared the sky: 'Fair weather cometh out of the north' (Job 37:22, KJV). We can imagine a garden under a sky covered by clouds preventing the heat of the sun getting through. In a similar way, a believer can be aware of spiritual clouds that prevent him fully sensing the presence of Jesus. These clouds may be sins, but they may not be. They can be anything that prevents clarity of spiritual vision. But they are beyond the abilities of even our renewed minds to deal with. We need the fresh input of the Spirit.

The south wind brought warmth and calm. This suggests that the disciple was agitated and needed solace. But the support she wanted was more than a calm which was devoid of heat. There is the danger of the spiritual equivalent of a stiff upper lip to control our spiritual concerns. While that may work for a while, it is not a pleasant or prolonged relief. The believer wants the calm that comes from the warm presence of the Comforter.

It is important to note why the believer wants the Spirit to come; the reason is that Jesus will be satisfied with him. Grace imparts to every believing soul the wonderful desire that Christ would be pleased with him. This desire is enhanced by recollections of previous visits by Jesus to our souls when he expressed his delight in us.

Having been prepared by the Spirit, the disciple now prays that Jesus would have fellowship with him.

The prompt answer of Jesus (5:1)

In 5:1, the woman anticipates a new meeting with the king: 'Let my beloved come to his garden, and eat its choicest fruits.' When the appropriate preparation has been done, he will always draw near. Her words are a reminder of the earnest desire of a spiritually-healthy Christian.

In response to her request, the king comes to the garden and there he gathers spices and eats some of its honey and drinks some of its wine. Jesus is depicted as greatly enjoying this visit to the heart of his disciple. The illustration is of him going round the garden gathering a sample from each plant. He does not miss out any of the items in the garden. Having gathered what he intends to feed on, he eats it along with wine (which is the symbol of joy).

Some of these plants are bitter (myrrh) and some are sweet (honey). The bitter ones may be the sad experiences that a believer is going through. If we are going through a difficult time in our garden, and we ask the Holy Spirit to blow upon it gently, Jesus will come to us and say, 'Your affliction is my affliction.' After all, he is our brother as well as our lover. He understands the distresses we go through. As it says in Isaiah 63:9: 'In all their affliction he was afflicted, and the angel of his presence saved them: in his love and in his pity he redeemed them; and he bare them, and carried them all the days of old.'(KJV)

On the other hand, we also have sweet experiences that are the equivalent of the honeycomb. These spiritual delights are usually found in the promises and other teachings of the Bible. Take, for example, a promise of heaven. It gives us great comfort and joy. But if we ask the Spirit to blow gently on our experience, Jesus will draw near and say, 'Your joy is my joy, because I too am looking forward to heaven.'

The visit of the king is not limited to his own participation – he exhorts others to eat and drink as much as they can take, indeed to keep on consuming until they are drunk with love. His visit illustrates how a visit from Jesus will ensure that other believers get benefit from the company of a believer who is enjoying a visit from Jesus. At the end of the verse, he exhorts the friends, whom I take to be the daughters of Jerusalem, the companions of the Bride, to share in the feast he is enjoying. These daughters depict other Christians and they get spiritual benefits through a spiritually-healthy believer's fellowship with Jesus.

Why does Jesus want these other believers to share in these blessings that he finds in the garden of a disciple's soul? The reason is that he wants them to provide him with these blessings in their own gardens. It is all very well to visit another garden and admire its beauty and receive a blessing. In addition, we should resolve to make all our gardens into places where Jesus can enjoy a feast and recommend its products to other believers.

POEM 7

SPIRITUAL RECOVERY (5:2–8:4)

She   ²I slept, but my heart was awake.
A sound! My beloved is knocking.
'Open to me, my sister, my love,
my dove, my perfect one,
for my head is wet with dew,
my locks with the drops of the night.'
³I had put off my garment;
how could I put it on?
I had bathed my feet;
how could I soil them?
⁴My beloved put his hand to the latch,
and my heart was thrilled within me.
⁵I arose to open to my beloved,
and my hands dripped with myrrh,
my fingers with liquid myrrh,
on the handles of the bolt.
⁶I opened to my beloved,
but my beloved had turned and gone.
My soul failed me when he spoke.
I sought him, but found him not;
I called him, but he gave no answer.
⁷The watchmen found me
as they went about in the city;
they beat me, they bruised me,
they took away my veil,
those watchmen of the walls.
⁸I adjure you, O daughters of Jerusalem,
if you find my beloved,
that you tell him
I am sick with love (5:2-8).

17

The Price of Refusal

SONG OF SOLOMON 5:2-8

The scene in this poem is totally different from the preceding one. There, under the picture of the king visiting his garden, we had seen Jesus and his disciple sharing happy fellowship. In this new scene, things are different. The varied scenes in this book are a reminder of the diverse nature of Christian experience and we are to learn lessons from each one because they depict experiences that we will encounter at some stage on our Christian pathway.

In these verses we have a poetic recounting of a dialogue between the woman and the daughters of Jerusalem after a refusal of the woman to let the king into her room. As we have suggested throughout, she depicts an individual believer, the daughters of Jerusalem are fellow disciples and the king is Jesus. In 5:2-8, the disciple informs the other believers of what has taken place, and closes by asking them to speak on her behalf should they see the king. They respond in 5:9 by asking her why her Beloved is so important and she responds in verses 10-16. Her admiring comments of her Beloved cause the daughters to desire to accompany her in locating him (6:1-3).

There are obvious spiritual lessons in this structure. Firstly, a disciple who has failed the Master in one way or another should enlist the help of other disciples. Secondly, these other disciples should aim to get the failed believer to stop speaking about her folly and instead to speak about Jesus. Thirdly, these disciples should volunteer to spend time with her until she has recovered her spiritual composure.

In this chapter, we will focus on 5:2-8, attempting to discover ways by which spiritual distance between Christ and us can come into our experience.

The condition of the disciple (v. 2)

The incident takes place at night, with the woman in bed. She describes herself as being asleep although her heart is awake. The king is not with her, he is outside. His absence makes her uneasy, which may be the reason why she cannot sleep deeply. The thoughts of her heart are keeping her from sleeping comfortably. What does this illustrate about Christian experience? She depicts a believer who has become separate from Christ in the sense that there is no active communion between him and her. This separation makes such a believer uneasy and his mind is restless.

We know that such experiences come our way for a variety of reasons. One reason is overtly sinful practices; when we fall into such activities, we will face the Lord's chastisement unless we repent of our sin. I don't think that is the picture of the disciple here, because the Beloved does not draw near to punish her. Instead he draws near to encourage her; therefore I would suggest that her spiritual state is one of satisfaction with the progress made. She is still able to discern his voice, which points to some possession of spiritual light. Yet her satisfaction is defective because she has lost the desire to proceed further.

The good feature of the situation is that the king knows about her problem and will not abandon her. There is a similar situation described in the letter to the church in Laodicea in Revelation 3. In that letter, Jesus describes his intention to come to the church in order to renew fellowship with willing disciples, even if the congregation in the main has abandoned fellowship with him.

The approach of the king (v. 2)
The woman recites the words of the king to her, and we can see them as words of Jesus. His appeal, to begin with, covers a wide perspective of the permanent relationship that there is between him and his follower. He mentions four details of the relationship. First, there is a family relationship -- they are brother and sister since both belong to the family of God. Second, there is a love relationship, similar to that of a married couple. Third, he mentions her dove-like features such as gentleness and peacefulness; he commends spiritual features that are developing in her character. Fourth, he says that she is without flaw in his sight (a reference to her justification). Each of these individual details is prefixed by 'my', which is a reminder of what her priority should be, the realisation that she belongs to him.

Secondly, the king says that he has made a journey in order to reach her location. This journey has been made through a wet night, depicting the efforts made by Jesus, often enduring uncongenial situations, in order to come and meet with his disciples. Sometimes we focus on the travels of the good Shepherd seeking lost sheep at their conversion and of the loving patience shown by him towards them at that time. We should not forget that often he has to show great determination and patience when seeking fellowship with his people long after their conversion.

So Jesus, when he draws near, reminds us of our spiritual privileges and of his willingness to make great efforts in order to restore us to active fellowship with him.

The attitude of the woman (vv. 3-4)
Initially the woman is reluctant to respond to the appeal of her Beloved for more time with her. It is remarkable how lethargic a Christian can become. In her current state, the

smallest action becomes unreasonable. It is amazing the number of frivolous reasons that can be made for not taking steps to meet with King Jesus. All the King has asked her to do is get up from the bed of satisfied ease and open the door. But she refuses. We can say that she prefers her comfort to communion with Jesus.

While she is lethargic and sluggish in responding, the king continues his attempt to have fellowship with her. It was usual for there to be large holes in doors that were used by those wanting entrance to a house or room; they would put a hand through the hole and open the latch. This is a reminder that Jesus has the ability to open the door of our hearts, if necessary; however, he prefers that his disciple would open the door for him.

When she saw his hand, she was deeply moved (the bowels were regarded as the seat of the emotions). What does his hand signify? She would have recalled what he had previously done with his hand. For example, she would recall that his hand had given her provision from his table, had guided her through his possessions (the garden and palaces), and had caressed her when she had fainted for love. The sight of his hand would have revived pleasant memories and created a desire for renewed experiences with him.

Her surprise at his absence (vv. 5-6)

So she rises to open the door. On the way she dips her hands in myrrh taken from one of the bottles containing fragrances that would have been in her room. She would have done this to make herself attractive to the king. Yet when she opens the door, he is not there, and she is devastated. Here we have a picture of a common Christian experience, that of discovering that sometimes Jesus absents himself at unusual times.

Her actions here of rising from the bed and the putting on of myrrh depict repentance. Repentance is an active grace and does involve believers leaving their places of illegitimate rest. Often this repentance is a sore experience in a spiritual sense and the believer may have a sense of crushing (myrrh was a fragrance produced from a crushed substance). Yet at the same time, such repentance has a sweet smell. As the believer moves to open to the Saviour, she will be saying to herself, 'How foolish I was in delaying to open.' And the extent of that folly she is about to discover. Jesus, who had been asking for fellowship, is not there now that she wants to meet him. He had withdrawn and she was distressed. Why does Jesus withdraw himself from a penitent disciple? One reason is for her to appreciate the folly of her action, another reason is to test the genuineness of her new desire.

Her searching for her Beloved (vv. 6-7)
The poem now describes her search for him. She begins looking for him near to the house before moving out into the city. I think this illustrates a believer searching for Jesus in private means of grace (prayer, meditation, self-examination) and then in public means of grace (the roads of the city are like various sources of public blessing: preaching, sacraments, fellowship).

She found him *silent* in the private means (v. 6). Is this not often our experience? For example, we read a promise in the Bible and desire to experience its power; we pray earnestly and persistently, yet something is lacking. We discover that the means of grace are not the same as Christ himself.

She found *seriousness* in the church. In a previous encounter, the watchmen had helped her when she was looking for Jesus (3:3-4). But on this occasion, the result was different: 'they beat me, they bruised me, they took away my veil, those watchmen of the walls.' Some commentators find fault with the watchmen here. They suggest that they depict ministers who are insensitive to the sad state of the disciple who is seeking for Jesus through the public means. No doubt, Christ's servants can be in a wrong state of soul and misread a situation. Yet

I suspect that while we should look at the watchmen as depicting ministers we should do so from another point of view. They wound a believer in the sense that they stress to her the solemnity of her sin in showing lethargy to Jesus. He enables his watchmen to speak appropriate words to her condition of soul. Her repentance is to be made deeper, although it will result in painful awareness. As she listens to them, she becomes aware of a sense of shame (to remove a woman's veil in public was to disgrace her). Her sins are uncovered by the watchmen. This does not mean that the watchmen should be cruel or unkind. But part of their role is to cause the citizens of Zion to have *intelligent* repentance when they have sinned.

Her response also indicates development in humility. She is willing to be rebuked, even though it causes her pain. It was her pride that had caused her to imagine that she did not need communion with Jesus; it is her humility that acknowledges that she had been wrong.

What we see here is the consequences of spiritual laziness of any kind in a Christian. Failure to respond to the loving appeal of Jesus may lead to his withdrawal, and this withdrawal can continue even after the believer has regained a measure of spiritual health. The biggest danger to our spiritual fervour may not be the glaring sins that do not attract us but the little sins that merely affect us a little.

Her sharing of her desire (v. 8)
There is one other source of help for her. At a time when personal devotions cannot locate Jesus, and when his servants are deepening her repentance, she is to turn to fellow-disciples for comfort. This is illustrated by the words of the woman to the daughters of Jerusalem. She wants them to bring her case to the king, which is a clear picture of a seeking disciple asking other believers to pray for her. Her message for Jesus is that her love for him is revived and needs to be communicated to him. As yet she does not have joy restored to her, but her love has returned. Love, whether

in recovery or in continued development, is not a grace that goes inward but outward, towards either Jesus or his people.

Here we see a *method for gracious recovery* for a sluggish Christian soul. First, there is personal repentance (depicted in her leaving the bed); second, there is persistent resolve (seen in her use of private means, of public means, and of brotherly intercession). If that is where we are, keep on searching.

Here we see *a miracle of grace*. Her separation from him, described at the beginning of the poem, had *reduced* her love for him. His separation from her, in response to her failure, had *increased* her love for him.

Others: ⁹What is your beloved more than another beloved,
O most beautiful among women?
What is your beloved more than another beloved,
that you thus adjure us?

She: ¹⁰My beloved is radiant and ruddy,
distinguished among ten thousand.
¹¹His head is the finest gold;
his locks are wavy,
black as a raven.
¹²His eyes are like doves
beside streams of water,
bathed in milk,
sitting beside a full pool.
¹³His cheeks are like beds of spices,
mounds of sweet-smelling herbs.
His lips are lilies,
dripping liquid myrrh.
¹⁴His arms are rods of gold,
set with jewels.
His body is polished ivory,
bedecked with sapphires.
¹⁵His legs are alabaster columns,
set on bases of gold.
His appearance is like Lebanon,
choice as the cedars.
¹⁶His mouth is most sweet,
and he is altogether desirable.
This is my beloved and this is my friend,
O daughters of Jerusalem (Song 5:9-16).

18

Love to an Unseen Christ

Song of Solomon 5:9-16

We saw in our previous study that the disciple of Jesus had behaved foolishly when Jesus had approached her looking for fellowship. Instead of getting up to let him in, she had preferred to remain in her comfortable bed. That comfortable bed pictures anything that a believer may prefer to have instead of fresh fellowship with Jesus, so it can even picture satisfaction with already-attained spirituality. Eventually, on seeing his hand trying to open the door, she arose and prepared herself by putting myrrh on her hands, which depicts the bitterness that accompanies repentance. Yet when she opened the door, he was gone.

This led to her searching for him, which is a reminder that Christian repentance is not merely satisfied with admitting one's fault; in addition the penitent believer wants restored fellowship. So she looks for Jesus first around her home, which illustrates a believer using the private means of grace such as prayer and meditation on the Bible. She still senses that full fellowship has not been restored, so she searches for him in the city, which pictures the church. There the watchmen found her (which illustrates the alertness of Christian ministers), and wounded her (which describes their pointing out to her the folly of her actions – repentance must be intelligent). Still she senses that full fellowship has not been restored. Therefore she makes her way to a third means of help and contacts the daughters of Jerusalem, that is, other believers.

The particular action that she wanted them to do for her was to pray for her when they next had fellowship with Jesus (5:8). Her request was that they tell him that she is sick with love. This is an interesting perspective on Christian honesty among believers. Often we don't admit that we are failing to obtain fresh fellowship with Jesus. We admit that we love him, but we don't indicate to one another that we want more. It is like a woman away from home with friends who tells them that she loves her husband but when she phones him she cannot get through to hear his voice.

Her request also gives insight into how we should describe one another as we pray for one another. Our appeal to the Master on the behalf of a seeking disciple should at times refer to her longing for love, not merely to have her love strengthened (which is important), but for her to enjoy visitations of love from Jesus. We should pray to Jesus that he would come and bless her.

Of course, these other believers recognise that the restored disciple is in need of spiritual comfort. So while they wait for their prayer for her to be answered, they do two things. First, they ask her to describe her Beloved (5:9-15) and, second, they offer to help find the Beloved (6:1-3). The first action is very important because it enables the disciple to cease focussing on herself and her folly. 'It is a good diversion under a deserted condition, and a suitable way to an outgate, to be dwelling rather upon the excellency of Christ than on the countless aggravations of our own sad condition; this is more honourable to Christ, more edifying to others, and more pleasant to ourselves.'[1] The second action is encouraging because it is a sign to the restored disciple that she is accepted by the other disciples.

---

[1] James Durham, pp. 293-94.

Yet there is another important lesson here, which is that believers can learn a great deal from restored backsliders. John Bunyan, in his book on the intercession of Christ, mentions that it is important for other Christians to observe the grace that has been shown to a backslider by Jesus. 'The returning backslider, therefore, is a rare man, a man of worth and intelligence, a man to whom the men of the world should flock, and of whom they should learn to fear the Lord God. He also is a man of whom the saints should receive both caution, counsel, and strength in their present standing; and they should, by his harms, learn to serve the Lord with fear, and to rejoice with trembling.'[2]

Her description of the Beloved (vv. 10-16)

In response to the question of the daughters, the woman proceeds to give a detailed and extensive description of her Beloved. In some ways, it is similar to the description of Jesus given in Revelation 1. It is evident that she knows him well.

Repentance enables recollection of previous experiences. When she was lying on her bed of ease she did not have the same capacity for describing her Beloved. Being now in a state of repentance, she recalls what she knows about him. Her description focuses on his perfections. A penitent believer wants a perfect Saviour. But she does not merely focus on his perfection in its entirety, as it were; she also examines his perfection in its parts. A lover will want to know all that is possible to know about the object of his love; so it is with a vibrant believer.

Jesus is healthy. The disciple says that her Beloved is 'white and ruddy'. Several commentators take these two colours as depicting his holiness (white) and his sacrifice (red blood). I suspect it points more to his permanent health. His healthful situation is further described as being one where he is 'the chief among ten thousand', words that point to a standard

---

[2] John Bunyan (1998), *The Intercession of Christ*, Christian Focus, p. 99.

bearer. Such a description points to a place of exaltation. We know that the risen Jesus now possesses fullness of life, in possession of an indestructible life, in the place of supreme elevation.

Of course, this interpretation is based on fuller New Testament light. In itself, this is not a problem because this is how the Old Testament should be interpreted. The authority we have for this approach is the method used by the Master himself in Luke 24:44: 'These are my words that I spoke to you while I was still with you, that everything written about me in the Law of Moses and the Prophets and the Psalms must be fulfilled.' While believers in Old Testament times would have had their interpretation as they anticipated the coming Messiah and perhaps grasped for an understanding, we can see in this description a beautiful picture of the risen Saviour.

Connected to his healthy experience is his youthful one: his head is tanned (like gold) and his hair is black. Again this can apply to the type of life possessed now by the risen Christ. Psalm 110, speaking of the king-priest after the order of Melchisedek, says that 'he has the dew of his youth'. The role of Jesus as king and priest is fulfilled in his exalted state. There he possesses fullness of life. This is not only a life that does not deteriorate, but it is a life that is suitable for its environment in heaven.

The next feature that is mentioned is the dove-like eyes of the Beloved. Obviously a dove points to peacefulness and gentleness, which are most attractive aspects of the Saviour's character. As the risen man, Jesus possesses the fruit of the Spirit. The eyes are further described as being white (this could be the significance of the reference to milk, indicating health) and wet (rivers of water). While tears are often a symptom of sadness, they can also indicate tender sympathy. Jesus gazes on his people with serenity, delight or concern, depending on their situation on their Christian journey.

The reference to the cheeks looking like a bed of spices or flowers seems to be another picture of the health of the Beloved. It has been observed that the cheeks are near the ear, and that this is a reference to the pleasure she gets by knowing that he listened to her words of love as she drew near him on previous occasions. His ears open to her words as flowers open to the light. This suggestion balances with the reference to his lips, which would be a description of his speaking to her previously. His words are fragrant like myrrh, and if this allusion to myrrh includes crushing, then here Jesus speaks to his disciple about the blessings that he can communicate through his sufferings on the cross.

This is followed by descriptions of his hands, belly and legs that point to his strength; he looks like a mighty cedar of Lebanon. The risen Jesus possesses all power. There is nothing that he cannot do. Just as the strength of a strong man is at the disposal of his wife, so the strength of the risen Jesus is there to be utilised by his people against their enemies.

The woman then says that his mouth is most sweet. This refers to the kisses that she would have received in the past. A kiss is an expression of intimacy, a special communication or display of love. In the past, this backsliding disciple had known sweet moments of assurance when her Beloved had drawn near and embraced her soul.

Having detailed these various features of her Beloved, she turns to her fellow-believers and declares that he is altogether lovely. She has no criticism to make of the way he has acted in response to her refusal to have fellowship with him. But her assurance has been increased by speaking about him because she describes him as her personal Beloved and Friend. The strategy of the daughters of Jerusalem has worked. The backsliding disciple continues on the road to meeting Jesus. And her words must have been sweet to Jesus' ear. She was closer to his cheeks than she imagined!

Why can we often not say this?

The answer may be that we are still in our beds. We are marked by spiritual inactivity; we don't make time for fellowship with him. Perhaps we did not profit from previous visits. Think of any activity you did this week. I don't mean your daily work, but an optional activity or interest. Did you spend more time doing it than you spent thinking about Jesus and speaking to him? I know many Christians who can absorb two hours of news a day or two hours of sport or two hours of television – but they don't spend two hours with Jesus. Would we have won our spouses if we had spent such little time with them?

Or we may be marked by religious activity that falls short of engaging with Christ. For example, it is possible to spend a lot of time reading about a particular doctrine that is under attack. One recent notion has been the openness of God, which denies that God has planned the future. I'm surprised that Christians bother to read books about it because the Bible clearly says that he has planned the future. Reading such books does not bring us to the feet of Jesus.

Or we may focus on a right doctrine but not link it sufficiently with Jesus. Every doctrine connected to our salvation is linked to Christ. Take the doctrine of adoption, which describes a state in which we have a right to all the privileges of the sons of God. But why do we have the right or why are we able to enjoy the privileges? Because they are connected to Jesus. We are adopted into the same family as him and are joint-heirs with him. With every doctrine, we should relate it to Jesus. (Of course, a similar attitude should be taken concerning our relationship with the Father and our relationship with the Spirit.)

Or it is because we have not repented as depicted in this poem. It is possible for us to realise that we are not what we should be, but then to remain where we are. Repentance is appropriate for believers as some of the messages to the seven churches in Revelation 2 and 3 indicate. Jesus there gave great promises to the churches, but the enjoyment of these promises depended on their repentance for failing to have been what they should have been.

Daughters: ¹Where has your beloved gone,
O most beautiful among women?
Where has your beloved turned,
that we may seek him with you?

She: ²My beloved has gone down to his garden
to the beds of spices,
to graze in the gardens
and to gather lilies.
³I am my beloved's and my beloved is mine;
he grazes among the lilies (Song 6:1-3).

19

Seeking Jesus Together

SONG OF SOLOMON 6:1-3

We come now to the second question asked by the daughters of Jerusalem in response to the request of the woman, who had failed to respond appropriately to the king's overture of love, which was that they should tell him that she is longing to experience again his love. That request depicts a recovering believer enlisting the prayer support of other Christians, which is obviously an essential Christian activity.

The daughters responded with more than prayer for her. First, they asked her to express what was significant about her Beloved. As we noted in the previous study, this request caused her to stop thinking about her spiritual folly and to focus instead on the beauties of the king. Her description revealed a heart full of love, and the description illustrates the heart a Christian has for Jesus. When such a one articulates her love for Jesus, she discovers that her assessment of him is an encouragement that she is going in the right direction as well as indicating to fellow believers that her repentance is genuine.

The woman's initial request had been asked because she had expected the daughters to know where the Beloved was. As fellow disciples they deduced from her answer to the first question that she was in a spiritually healthy state, in fact able to show them where the Beloved was. Their outlook is a marvellous picture of how grace in spiritually-healthy believers should accept the rapid progress of grace in a restored backslider. Often we want to put such a disciple through a process of prolonged testing before we accept their usefulness again. Yet several biblical examples point to a different response.

Think of David in Psalm 51, which is the written expression of his repentance over his sins connected to his adultery with Bathsheba. He expects that his restoration to fellowship with his God will lead to soon, if not immediate, usefulness; he says in verses 12-13: 'Restore to me the joy of your salvation, and uphold me with a willing spirit. Then I will teach transgressors your ways, and sinners will return to you.' It is the case that David was backsliding for over a year, but the process of restoration was quick.

Another example of biblical restoration is found in 2 Corinthians 2 regarding a person who had been disciplined by the congregation on the instructions of Paul. (It is not clear if the disciplined person is the same individual mentioned in 1 Corinthians 5; if it is, then less than a year has passed since his discipline for grievous sins.) The disciplinary process has worked because the offending brother has repented of his sin. Therefore Paul writes in 2 Corinthians 2:6-8: 'For such a one, this punishment by the majority is enough, so you should rather turn to forgive and comfort him, or he may be overwhelmed by excessive sorrow. So I beg you to reaffirm your love for him.' How long should discipline last for? Until the goal has been obtained – the goal of repentance. There is no benefit in continuing to discipline a penitent disciple.

Another detail of the daughters' question should be noted. They repeat their description of her that they gave in the first question (5:9): 'Fairest among women.' Of course, it is appropriate to say that her beauty is that which is shared by all believers – the beauty of the righteousness of Christ. Yet to suggest this meaning is probably to ignore the more appropriate interpretation which is that healthy believers see great beauty in the gracious repentance of a backsliding Christian. People admire the melting snow on a mountain, watching the rivers of water make their way down the slope. However marvellous that sight is, it is nothing in comparison to the beauty of the tears on the face of a penitent disciple.

People are asked by the advertising world to use various products to help them display their beauty, be it clothes or fragrances or whatever. When we gather in church, we enter a different type of beauty contest. We should reveal the hidden beauty of the heart, and the one that is described here is the beauty of repentance. I remember hearing an elderly Christian being asked what he thought was the big difference between the Christianity he had seen when he was younger and the Christianity he observed in his old age. His answer was, 'Lack of tears.'

I suppose another reason that can be deduced from the question of the daughters is that they were personally aware that in themselves they were not more qualified to find the Beloved than their friend was. Although they may not have backslidden in the manner that she had done, they were aware of their own faults, and did not want to separate themselves into a separate class of believer from her. They needed her help in locating the Beloved.

The answer of the disciple (6:2-3)
The woman informs the daughters that the Beloved has gone into his garden. This was the place where she and the Beloved, accompanied by the daughters, had previously enjoyed each other's company (1:16–2:3). Sometimes in the Song the garden depicts a location, while in other references it describes the individual believer's heart (4:16). Here, given that the daughters are going to accompany her, it illustrates the location where more than one believer enjoys fellowship with Jesus, which is the public means of grace. The garden depicts the people of God as they meet in public.

As we noted in a previous study, the garden of the king was large, more like an estate, and in it there were several smaller gardens (this explains the use of the singular 'garden' in the first clause and the plural 'gardens' in the second clause). Out of the variety of vegetation and flowers in this garden, she mentions the beds of spices and the lilies.

I would suggest that the beds in which the spices are found depict the various means of grace, with the spices describing the variety of benefits that come to the Lord's people through using these beds. Just as in the image of the city, where the streets and houses illustrate means of grace, so in the image of the garden the beds depict these several means. There is the bed of preaching, there is the bed of prayer, there is the bed of the Lord's Supper, and there is the bed of fellowship. I suspect that each bed contains the same spices, indicating that the effect of participating in each will give to Christians the same benefits as they find in the other beds.

A list of these spices is given in 4:13-14: '...henna with nard, nard and saffron, calamus and cinnamon, with all trees of frankincense, myrrh and aloes, with all choice spices.' They picture the variety of graces that come our way through participating in the means of grace. Our love is deepened, our faith is warmed, our hope is strengthened, our peace is increased, our joy is intensified, our gentleness is developed, our patience is fortified, and our repentance is sweetened. In these beds of spices, we receive the Saviour's instructions, read about his promises, discover his desires for us, and enjoy fellowship with him.

The Beloved also feeds in the gardens. What food does he find there? No doubt, in the church he enjoys the company of his friends; he feeds on them as he anticipates the time when the beds of spices will be done away; he notices with delight the fruit of the Spirit in their lives, and while he desires that they will increase in grace, he is also content with their company. On this particular occasion, he is feeding on the repentance of the restored backslider, on her desires for him; he is also enjoying the company of her fellow believers who are helping her in her quest.

In this garden, the Beloved gathers lilies. As we noticed regarding previous references in the Song, the lilies probably depict the purity (whiteness) and humility (drooping head) of the believers. I suppose we can say that the Beloved, in addition to appreciating their beauty in the garden (sanctification), is also gathering lilies into his garden and collecting lilies from his garden. He gathers lilies *into* the garden through the preaching of the gospel. That is one of the means of grace in which unbelievers are blessed. This is one of the delights of the heavenly Gardener to transform weeds of the world into lilies and transplant them into his garden. There is not a weed that is too noxious for Jesus to change into a lily. It is wonderful to observe our Beloved carrying into the garden a former weed now become a flower. How gently and gladly he does so. The Gardener takes each of these lilies into his church in a way that is special to each.

He gathers lilies *from* his garden when he removes them to another garden, to the heavenly Paradise. In his love, he gently removes them and carries them to heaven and plants them where they can permanently and fully enjoy the sunshine of his love and the copious ministrations of the Holy Spirit, who gave them foretastes of heaven as they visited the beds of spices in the earthly garden.

Restored assurance

There is one other benefit from this visit to the garden, which is that the disciple obtains great assurance of her relationship to her Beloved (v. 3). She affirms that she is his and he is hers. Obviously these words point to a mutual relationship in which they experience one another and respond to one another.

Individual assurance that had begun in her use of private means of grace is strengthened by using the public means. In the preceding chapter, which describes the process of her restoration, she was aware that he was her Beloved because she calls him 'my Beloved' several times. Penitent believers often become aware that Jesus is theirs while still being concerned whether or not they are as delightful to him as they were before their period of backsliding. Through going to the garden and utilising the beds of spices and observing the Gardener gathering lilies, she had restored to her soul the wonderful realisation that Jesus still thought highly of her.

In her visit to the garden, the disciple was able to give herself once again to Jesus. This dedication should be a feature of all our visits there. But she discovered that Jesus was also determined to give himself and all that he has to her. Although she had refused his nearness previously, she was assured that he would come and share his blessings with her. Perhaps this is why she puts first what she means to him. On a previous occasion she had reversed the order (2:16), but on that occasion she was not a recovering backslider.

Why are there times when we do not possess assurance? Perhaps we have not used the varied means of grace that the disciple used to get out of her frame of spiritual lethargy. Perhaps we don't spend long enough at each of the beds of spices and don't observe the Gardener gathering his lilies.

The King: ⁴You are beautiful as Tirzah, my love,
lovely as Jerusalem,
awesome as an army with banners.
⁵Turn away your eyes from me,
for they overwhelm me –
Your hair is like a flock of goats
leaping down the slopes of Gilead.
⁶Your teeth are like a flock of ewes
that have come up from the washing;
all of them bear twins;
not one among them has lost its young.
⁷Your cheeks are like halves of a pomegranate
behind your veil.
⁸There are sixty queens and eighty concubines,
and virgins without number.
⁹My dove, my perfect one, is the only one,
the only one of her mother,
pure to her who bore her.
The young women saw her and called her blessed;
the queens and concubines also, and they praised her.

The Attendants:
¹⁰'Who is this who looks down like the dawn,
beautiful as the moon, bright as the sun,
awesome as an army with banners?'
(Song 6:4-10).

20

The King's Opinion of a Restored Backslider

Song of Solomon 6:4-10

We saw in previous studies how the woman endeavoured to locate the king whose presence she had lost through laziness, by preferring to remain in bed instead of arising and letting him in. Having realised her folly, she endeavoured to find him but had failed, and we noted that this was a picture of a restored believer attempting to re-discover Jesus through both the private and public means of grace. She then enlisted the help of her fellow believers (the daughters of Jerusalem) who realised that she was no longer a backslider and therefore asked her suitable questions designed to help her recognize her restored situation. They also realised that she knew where the king would be even though she had not realised she possessed that knowledge. Upon discovering where he was (in the garden, a picture of the visible church), they went there with her.

    I suppose we could ask here what the difference was between her searching for an absent Christ in the city where the watchmen humiliated her (a picture of Christ's servants highlighting for her the depth of her sinfulness) and her searching for him in the garden. The obvious difference is that she sought by herself in the city but she sought with other believers in the garden. This is a reminder to us that we are more liable to enjoy fellowship with Jesus when we seek him together with other Christians. Of course, Jesus will reveal himself to individuals if they are the only ones in a company who want to meet him, as was the case in the church in Laodicea.

I suspect we can also see in the woman's experience here a development in the experience of assurance. So far she possesses an aspect of personal assurance that can be described as deductive. There are two aspects of this deductive assurance that can be mentioned. First, she desires to meet with the Saviour whom she had known intimately on previous occasions, and this desire is evidence that she possesses genuine faith. A true desire to have fellowship with an absent Saviour verifies that the seeker is a true disciple, even though the absence was caused by her fault.

Second, she also had the form of assurance that comes from knowing the estimation of other spiritual people, depicted in the questions of the daughters of Jerusalem. The nature of their fellowship, in which they showed themselves willing to learn of her although she had failed so foolishly, would have encouraged her by reminding her that they still regarded her as a true believer. Mutual encouragement is very important.

But she needed more – she wanted assurance from Jesus himself. This is why she came to the garden (the public meeting of his church) with his people; this is why she went round the various beds (the means of grace) in the garden planted by the Gardener, her Beloved. And as she did so, he drew near and told her what he thought of her.

The king, in saying that she is beautiful, says three things about her and uses several images to illustrate her comeliness. Her beauty is made up of strength, health, and dignity.

The restored backslider possesses strength (v. 4)

Her strength is depicted by his reference to strong cities (Tirzah was city in Manasseh and Jerusalem was the capital) and to an army (v. 4). Cities in those days had walls round them to defend them from attack and I would suggest that his reference to them indicates that he regarded this restored backslider as being able to resist enemies that would attack her. His reference to an army could also point to defence, but I suspect it also balances the previous picture of defence and so is an illustration of being able to attack the positions of the enemy. Jesus says that the restored backslider is able to withstand spiritual enemies and destroy spiritual strongholds. We would probably be surprised if this was said of a Christian who had not backslidden because we know how weak every Christian is. So to hear it said of one who had fallen is surprising.

This form of thinking reminds us that often we forget that our stability and strength are totally dependent on divine grace. A Christian is not like a body builder who builds up present strength from past exercise. Of course, we learn wisdom and other ongoing benefits from previous experiences. But a victory yesterday is no guarantee of a victory today.

The examples of backsliders becoming stalwarts in the faith are many. In the previous chapter we thought of David, who fell so drastically, yet who declared in Psalm 51 that he will become an effective soldier if he is restored; he is confident that when he instructs others they will be converted and cease being enemies of the king. Another example is Peter, who was so weak against the devil's attacks at the time of Christ's arrest; yet he would become a rock, able to help others resist the devil.

This description of strong cities and an army reminds believers of an ever-present danger – their enemies are always on the prowl. Therefore they need to have on the spiritual armour that God has provided (Eph. 6:10ff.), they have to be strong as the young men to whom John wrote, who were strong because the word of God abided in them, with the result that they overcame the wicked one (1 John 2:14). The description also reminds believers of their duty, which is to pray constantly, 'Hold up my goings, Lord' (Ps. 17:5 KJV).

The restored backslider is healthy (vv. 5-6)

Jesus informs the restored backslider that she is healthy. He refers to her eyes, her hair and her teeth. He likens her hair to the hair of a goat and her white teeth to vigorous sheep. Even on an everyday level, we can tell that someone is healthy by looking at their eyes, hair and teeth. This is an important reminder to us that a restored backslider is not unhealthy.

The king here repeats the description he had given of the woman in 4:1-3, before she had experienced her sad fall. It is wonderful that his estimation of her is still the same, now that she has repented of her sin and rejoined her companions. 'Renewing of repentance and faith by believers after failings, puts them in that same condition and capacity with Christ, for laying claim to his love, and their wonted privileges and comforts, wherein they were before, even as if such failings and miscarriages had never been.'[1]

He does add one difference, which is the effect her eyes have on him. He says that her look overcomes him. What is so significant about her eyes now? Given that she is repenting, he is referring to the sorrow, to the tears that are seen in her eyes. Our eyes are very important. Peter tells us that we should have long vision, to see afar off, to be able to look ahead to the coming glory (2 Pet. 1:9). We are to set our vision on to heavenly things. But there is something better than having good spiritual eyesight – it is having good vision in a tearful eye. Before we fall, we may forget that heaven is ours only by grace; after we are restored from a spiritual fall, we again look at heaven and with tears say, 'Jesus is still going to give it to me.'

The king esteems penitent disciples (vv. 7-10)

The king says of this restored backslider that she means more to him than all the princely attendants round his throne. At a literal level, Solomon was surrounded by queens, concubines and other female servants, and this retinue would have accompanied him as he walked round his garden. But his

---

[1] James Durham (1840, 1997), *The Song of Solomon*, Banner of Truth, p. 345.

The King's Opinion of a Restored Backslider

affections are towards this penitent woman. At a far higher level, Jesus is surrounded by heavenly servants who are marked by dignity and purity — the angelic host. But Jesus loves his repentant disciple more than that he does the heavenly host, and the sound of her sobbing voice is more pleasant than all the eloquence of these heavenly beings.

What does he say about her? First, she is still a dove; second, she is unique (she is the only child of her mother); third, she is praised by the attendants. This penitent backslider still has the features of a dove that she possessed before (gentleness, peacefulness, good eyesight, peace). Her uniqueness is highlighted; even a backslider is different from all other people because he or she is still a child of God, and that uniqueness is never lost.

The garden is a picture of the church, of God's people gathered together to benefit from the various means of grace. When they meet in public worship, they meet with Jesus, their king. In the gathering are some of the heavenly host (1 Cor. 11:10). They learn about their God as they watch his people (Eph. 3:10). When they see backsliders joining with other believers to worship God, the heavenly retinue once more see the amazing grace of God.

The opinion of the heavenly host is depicted here in the words of the attendants (v. 10) — they praise the repentant disciple in the sense that they admire the blessings that grace has brought into her life. As they see her with the king, they compare her to what is clear and bright – the sun and the moon (v. 10). They know the defects that she had experienced; nevertheless they can see that forgiveness and restoration result in a beautiful Christian, ready to advance the Lord's cause as a soldier in his army. It was common in the ancient world for appropriate words to be written on banners: on the banners of this believer are written 'forgiven by Jesus', 'restored by Jesus', 'still loved by Jesus'.

Don't look down on restored believers – Jesus thinks they are beautiful. So do the heavenly host!

The king   [11]I went down to the nut orchard
to look at the blossoms of the valley,
to see whether the vines had budded,
whether the pomegranates were in bloom.
[12]Before I was aware, my desire set me
among the chariots of my kinsman, a prince.
[13]Return, return, O Shulammite,
return, return, that we may look upon you.
Why should you look upon the Shulammite,
as upon a dance before two armies?
(Song 6:11-13).

21

The Explanation of the King

SONG OF SOLOMON 6:11-13

There is disagreement as to who is speaking in these verses, with some arguing that it is the woman whereas others say it is the king. The decision as to the speaker must be made from the content of the verses. Moody Stuart, who regards the woman as the speaker, says that these words indicate her longing for the coming of spring, for signs of life, for evidence that the Spirit has returned to her. As she did so, she found herself being drawn speedily into the king's presence (v. 12).[1] This interpretation means that the speakers in verse 13 are the daughters of Jerusalem. They saw the woman seeking for the Messiah and were attracted to her; they further want to see her attractiveness now[2] she has found him again. What they will see is likened to two armies, which Moody Stuart says is a picture of the spiritual conflict in the believer.

What that author describes is certainly a picture of Christian experience. Yet two details in the description point

---

1 Alexander Moody Stuart (1857), *The Song of Songs*, James Nisbet, p. 493.
2 Ibid., 497-99.

to the speaker not being the woman. First, it would be very surprising that other disciples (the speakers in v. 13) would ask her to leave the king's presence (after all, this is where they wanted her to be). Second, it is not obvious that the reference to two armies points to a battle within the woman. Therefore, I want to look at the passage to see if the speaker can be the king.

In the context, as we saw in the previous study, the penitent disciple has returned to the King's presence along with her fellow believers. She has come to the garden which we suggested is an illustration of the church with its variety of means of grace. She has heard him there describe her as spiritually strong, healthy and unique. He continues to speak, and we have to ask to what is he referring. When did he go to his garden to see the condition of the various items in it?

I would suggest that he is speaking retrospectively. What these verses describe is what the king was doing during the time that his disciple was not in intimate contact with him. Since that evening, when she refused to open the door to let him in, we have been focussing on what the woman was doing as she sought to recover her lost intimacy. But what was he doing? He tells us in these verses. In verses 4-9, he gives his estimation of her as a restored backslider; in verses 11-13 he gives an explanation of where he went when she refused to let him enter on that occasion. He says that he went to his garden, the church.

The king here describes the garden as being full of abundant fruit. Its name (the Garden of Nuts) suggests that it was full of them, as well as being a vineyard and an orchard. The idea is that there was plenty fresh provision there for those who fed in it. In picture language, the Saviour says that when his disciple would not have fellowship with him he went to where communion could be enjoyed with other disciples. This is a reminder that Jesus does not become inactive merely because a disciple's spiritual energy is low. He has a garden that requires his constant care.

Although he went to the garden disappointed that she did not want his fellowship, he did not leave her in anger but in anticipation because he knew that eventually she would come there in the company of other disciples. Nevertheless, while he was in the garden he was overcome by a strong desire to be with her, a desire that would be speedily executed when she reappeared. He likens it to the speed of fast chariots. It is not clear whether the word translated 'Amminadib' in some versions is a proper name of a well-known charioteer or if it should be translated as 'chariots of the people of the Prince'. The imagery tells us three things. First, when a believer backslides, there is in the heart of Jesus a strong desire for her company. The Saviour misses one of his people when such a disciple is far away spiritually. Second, Jesus is always ready to respond quickly the moment that disciple comes to meet with him. Third, it indicates that Jesus is aware of the initial desires of the disciple to be restored to intimate fellowship with him.

Call for repentance (vv. 12-13)

In verse 12, the king mentions that he called to her to return in order that he and his companions could look upon her. Four times he cries out, 'Return.' While the repetition highlights the depth of longing in his heart, we must recall that the words of a king are always with power. This is the effectual working of the King of love, not merely imploring, but also enabling his backsliding disciple to come back to him. This is the secret as to why the disciple was so eager to find her King. She imagined she was initiating each of the stages in her recovery, whether in seeking him privately, or in the city, or enlisting the help of fellow disciples. But behind each scene, he was crying, 'Return.' This was why she found herself seeking for spiritual recovery.

Jesus can use different means in order to say 'return'. With David, he sent Nathan the prophet to say 'return'. With Peter, Jesus said 'Return to me' when his disciple turned and looked at him after his denial; he said 'Return to me' in every tear that Peter shed after he realised what he had done; and he said 'Return to me' when the angels told the women to go and tell Peter that the tomb was empty.

The king calls her by a very precious name. 'Shulammite' does not say much in English, but it is the feminine form of the name Solomon. He gives his own name to her, signifying that his assets are hers. We see a beautiful example of this in Jeremiah's use of the divine title, 'The Lord our righteousness.' In Jeremiah 23:6 he speaks of the days of the Messiah: 'In his days Judah will be saved, and Israel will dwell securely. And this is the name by which he will be called: "The Lord is our righteousness."' That is his divine title. Jeremiah uses very similar words in Jeremiah 33:16 about the same period, except he uses the same name of God's people: 'In those days Judah will be saved and Jerusalem will dwell securely. And this is the name by which it will be called: "The Lord is our righteousness."' Both Jesus and his people have the same name because they have been given his righteousness.

Another example of this sharing of names is found in 1 Corinthians 12:12-13: 'For just as the body is one and has many members, and all the members of the body, though many, are one body, so it is with *Christ*. For in one Spirit we were all baptized into one body — Jews or Greeks, slaves or free — and all were made to drink of one Spirit.' Both Jesus and his people are meant in Paul's usage of the term 'Christ' in verse 12.

As we know, Solomon means 'peace'. The environment of peace usually means the existence of no conflicts; if they increase, the enjoyment of peace is often lost. She had created a situation of conflict by her refusal to meet with him for fellowship. Yet Jesus says to her that although she was not enjoying his peace because of her folly, he still regarded her as being in a state of peace. He did not call her by this name after she was restored, but it was how he regarded her before she repented, during the period he was calling on her to return. A believer never loses the standing of justification which brings peace with God. Jesus never says about a backslider, 'I wish they did not have this status of peace with God.' Instead, he sees them as those who should be experiencing the inner peace that is given to those who have the standing of reconciliation with God.

Some verses from elsewhere in the Bible describe this desire of Jesus to give the experience of peace to backsliding disciples. Psalm 85:8: 'I will hear what God the LORD will speak: for he will speak peace unto his people, and to his saints: but let them not turn again to folly.' Isaiah 48:18: 'Oh that you had paid attention to my commandments! Then your peace would have been like a river, and your righteousness like the waves of the sea.' The disciples were in a bad state of soul in the upper room, but Jesus said to them in John 14.27 (KJV): 'Peace I leave with you, my peace I give unto you: not as the world giveth, give I unto you. Let not your heart be troubled, neither let it be afraid.' How great is the desire of Jesus that each of his people, including his penitent ones, should have his peace.

The fourfold use of the term 'return' also indicates the degree of welcome that penitent disciples will receive from Jesus. Of course, these meetings are often secret. I would like to have observed Jesus and Peter when they met on the Resurrection Day. But it is actually better to have our own experience of Christ's restoration than to have the privilege of observing another's restoration.

Why does he want her to return? He wants her restored so that he and his companions can look upon her. She now possesses great beauty because the grace of repentance has deepened in her heart. In every feature of her soul, sorrow for her sin has left its gracious effect. This is not morbidness; such a negative response to failure does not bring a person to repent. Instead, when Jesus and his companions see her, they see penitent love, penitent joy, penitent peace, penitent gentleness, penitent perseverance. It is a sight worth looking at.

Of course, we are not to imagine that there is only one penitent believer in the church. The truth is that a healthy, attractive church is composed entirely of penitent believers. Jesus says to us to return to him so that he and his companions in the garden, whether the daughters who accompanied her (fellow believers) or the retinue that accompanied him (the angelic host), could admire her beauty.

What will they see when she returns? It seems that the reference to 'a company of two armies' is to a dance that would take place when people gathered together. The people in general were not dancing; instead they observed mainly young women dancing. The picture seems to be that her happy experience of restoration is like the dance of joy that would take place when there were peaceful gatherings. Spiritual restoration is a time for great celebration, it takes place among the peaceful gatherings of God's people, and the restored person should be expressing joy. Her heart should be dancing with delight.

These verses teach us two important details. One is that Jesus, the spurned Lover, is involved in the process of his Beloved's recovery. The other is that a great welcome is given every time a backsliding believer returns. A backslider does not have to be a public sinner nor does backsliding describe only a long period away from Christ. It can happen in our hearts and may not last for long. Whatever its length, Christ should be given the praise for our recovery, and whatever its recurrence, we should rejoice in his wonderful welcome to us.

The king   ¹How beautiful are your feet in sandals,
O noble daughter!
Your rounded thighs are like jewels,
the work of a master hand.
²Your navel is a rounded bowl
that never lacks mixed wine.
Your belly is a heap of wheat,
encircled with lilies.
³Your two breasts are like two fawns,
twins of a gazelle.
⁴Your neck is like an ivory tower.
Your eyes are pools in Heshbon,
by the gate of Bath-rabbim.
Your nose is like a tower of Lebanon,
which looks toward Damascus.
⁵Your head crowns you like Carmel,
and your flowing locks are like purple;
a king is held captive in the tresses.
⁶How beautiful and pleasant you are,
O loved one, with all your delights!
⁷Your stature is like a palm tree,
and your breasts are like its clusters.
⁸I say I will climb the palm tree
and lay hold of its fruit.
Oh may your breasts be like clusters of the vine,
and the scent of your breath like apples,
⁹and your mouth like the best wine
(Song 7:1-9).

22

The King's Appreciation of her Beauty

SONG OF SOLOMON 7:1-9

In the previous section (6:11-13), the king had informed the woman as to what he was doing during the period when they were separated as a result of her refusal to have fellowship with him. He had gone down to the garden (the church) because he knew eventually she would return there. Her return would be achieved through his own endearing methods depicted in the fourfold use of the word 'return'.

Meanwhile, an aspect of his activity in the garden was to prepare other visitors to the garden for her return. These visitors we have identified as two groups: there are those who belong to the retinue of the king (they depict the angels) and there are the daughters of Jerusalem (her fellow believers). He says that when she returns to the garden, she will perform a dance before the observing groups and the king (6:13). This imagery depicts the joy of a restored disciple. The preparation was essential because the members of the groups were to experience a pleasant surprise. Instead of observing a suppressed, fearful disciple, they would see a liberated, rejoicing disciple.

In passing, we may note that dancing was part of the culture of Israel and it had both positive and negative usages in the Bible. *Positively*, when the army of Israel returned from their victories over their enemies, they were met by dancing women (1 Sam. 18:6). David danced before the Lord with all his might as the ark of the covenant came into Jerusalem (2 Sam. 6:14). Dancing is mentioned as part of the praise at the temple (Pss. 149:1-3; 150:4). Jeremiah, when predicting the restoration of Israel from captivity, describes the celebrations as including dancing (Jer. 31:13). Jesus described the joy associated with the returning prodigal as feasting along with music and dancing. *Negatively*, dancing occurred when the Israelites worshipped the golden calf (Exod. 32:19). It was a response to a dance that led to the execution of John the Baptist. Basically dancing was performed at occasions of public rejoicing and did not involve both sexes dancing together. Solomon is using a common situation to depict the manner of the return of a backslider.

Verses 1-9 are the descriptive words of the king as he, along with the retinue and the daughters of Jerusalem, watches her performance. His words indicate that he is greatly pleased by what he observes as he describes her beautiful appearance and fine movements.

Dignified title (v. 1)
Consider the dignified title that he gives her; he calls her a 'noble daughter' or 'prince's daughter' (a similar title – 'king's daughter' – occurs in Psalm 45:13, KJV). This title is not referring to her family background but to her current status. She had belonged to a family that kept vineyards (1:6), but now she belonged to royalty. Every disciple, including recovered backsliders, has this elevated status of belonging to the family of God. As the king observes the joy of his restored disciple, he enhances her assurance by addressing her according to her present status and not according to her previous folly.

As already noted, this long poem within the Song is concerned with a repentant believer and the manner of her restoration. When she spurned his fellowship, she found herself without the personal assurance that she longed for. She is now back in conscious fellowship with the king, but given her folly we might anticipate words of rebuke, perhaps an allusion to where she came from as being the reason for her unseemly behaviour. It is true that the reason why we refuse to have fellowship with Christ is because of our remaining sin. The connection we have to our old family (of Adam) prevents us from enjoying the privileges of our new family (of Christ). It is not surprising that when we have recovered from times of backsliding, we anticipate being reminded of our past. Yet the king instead stressed her permanent position as a prince's daughter.

Part of our problem is that we have great difficulty, even as believers, of appreciating the wonder of grace. We find it hard to accept that restoration means restoration. Instead we imagine that there has to be a lengthy process of penitence after we have repented, by which we earn the right to be once again addressed as 'Prince's daughter'. We can accept that we are forgiven, but seem to listen to the language of the prodigal son ('I am no longer worthy to be called your son') instead of listening to the words of the father ('Bring quickly the best robe, and put it on him, and put a ring on his hand, and shoes on his feet. And bring the fattened calf and kill it, and let us eat and celebrate. For this my son was dead, and is alive again; he was lost, and is found,' Luke 15:22-24).

As a prince's daughter, she has great privileges. She belongs to a wealthy Master, she has his resources to meet her needs, and she has his promises to maintain her sense of security. Although she is subject to him, she is not merely a servant. In addition to her responsibilities to live according to the family name, she possesses the blessings that accompany the relationship. And she is discovering that she is never cast out of his family, even when she behaves foolishly. This is the experience of all believers. They sin and turn away from Jesus for one reason or another. He brings them to repentance, and when they return to his presence they hear him say to each of them, 'Prince's daughter.' He doesn't reduce their status because they have sinned. They are not children on a lower level of sonship than those who haven't sinned (the latter group does not exist, of course).

Delightful spectacle (vv. 1-7)

The poem depicts the woman as performing a dance. There are two details of this picture that stand out: one is the harmony of movement and the other is the beauty of every part. Obviously, when a person dances well, the hands, feet, head and eyes work together. If one of these body parts fails, then the movements of the whole are impaired. Just as in a physical dance, so the dance of the heart requires the contribution of all its parts. The mind, the emotions and the will have to be involved. Because she has been instructed or enlightened regarding the fullness of restoration, she understands how she has been treated. She is aware of the welcome, of the forgiveness, of the forgetting of her folly by her Beloved. Having grasped this wonderful reality, her emotions are affected. Her love is increased, her peace is overflowing, her joy is boundless. With her mind and heart working together, her will joins in and she expresses what she knows and loves. As we look at her, we see the attractiveness of each part and the beauty of the whole.

The king gives expression to his delight by comparing the various features of her body to notable sites and locations. (It has been observed that he mentions ten of her features, which is the same number of features that she had mentioned of him in 5:10-16; this number points to the attention to detail that each had given to the other.) I don't think we have to identify precise spiritual meanings to her ankles, her waist, her head or the other body parts. The writer is using the actions of a physical body to depict the spiritual movement of the heart of a believer who is enjoying the grace of restoration. His point is that the Beloved enjoys observing the details in each faculty of her penitent soul. He sees nothing unbecoming in her; indeed he is transfixed by her (he is bound by her beauty, v. 5).

As we suggested, the woman is being observed by the two groups as well as by the King. They also observed his delight in her. Beautiful lessons are taught in the garden to the King's heavenly retinue and to the restored backslider's companions.

Determined affection (vv. 8-9)
Having watched this wonderful activity by the disciple, the king intimates his intention to enjoy her company. Through this imagery we are being told that Jesus desires fellowship with such a disciple. As he promised the overcomer in the spiritually-bankrupt church of Laodicea, so he informs his disciple that he will draw near to her. She is not only going to enjoy his company when others are present, but she is going to discover that there will be personal communion as well. In a sense, Jesus says in these verses that he is going to do what she had prevented him doing when she had refused to let him in when he knocked at her door. In her company, he will find rest and refreshment.

She   9It goes down smoothly for my beloved,
gliding over lips and teeth.
10I am my beloved's,
and his desire is for me.
11Come, my beloved,
let us go out into the fields
and lodge in the villages;
12let us go out early to the vineyards
and see whether the vines have budded,
whether the grape blossoms have opened
and the pomegranates are in bloom.
There I will give you my love.
13The mandrakes give forth fragrance,
and beside our doors are all choice fruits,
new as well as old,
which I have laid up for you, O my beloved
(Song 7:9-13).

23

The Restored Disciple's Desire for Fellowship

SONG OF SOLOMON 7:9-13

The woman has listened with delight to the king's description of her beauty and to his words of longing to know her more intimately. This was the case despite her sad backsliding, but now that she had returned to him in repentance, he has affirmed that she is lovely in his sight. 7:9b to 8:4 describe her response to his words in 7:1-9a. She begins her response by taking up his allusion to wine in which he connected her mouth to the best wine. His illustration depicted the beauty of her words, and now she gives an example of them, as she indicates how freely they flowed.

Assurance that is experienced by a restored backslider (v. 10)

In verse 10, the woman speaks to herself. She has listened with delight to what the king had said and now she addresses her own heart. Her response is a picture of a believer applying Christ's words to herself, ensuring that they are engraved into her spiritual outlook. The first clause, 'I am my Beloved's,' is a recognition by the disciple that she belongs to Jesus. There are several ways in which a disciple belongs to Jesus. First, she belongs to him as a result of the eternal counsels in which the Father gave a people to his

207

Son, with the intent that he should redeem them from sin. Second, she belongs to him because he purchased her with his blood when he paid the penalty on the cross for her sins. She had forgotten that he owned her when she had refused to let him in (Song 5:3). Yet having being restored from her backsliding she realises afresh that she belongs to him. It is the case that a recovered backslider has great insight into spiritual realities. Third, she was his also because she had dedicated herself to him when they first met. With joy she had believed the gospel invitation and discovered his warm welcome into his family. Sadly this dedication had waned until she declined his company on that sad occasion mentioned in the previous paragraph. Now she has realised that he is welcoming her into his fellowship and therefore she gladly responds with a fresh statement of dedication.

In what manner would she have said this statement? No doubt there would be a sense of wonder at the grace the King had shown to her in forgiving her sin and restoring her. Along with the sense of wonder there would also be humility because of his willingness to associate with her, so unworthy of his affections. Accompanying the wonder and the humility would be delight that she was experiencing his grace. These three responses are not surprising from a forgiven backslider, but perhaps another response that she gives would not be expected, the response of anticipation of his company.

Boldness displayed by a restored backslider (vv. 11-13)

In verse 11 she suggests that they go together on a journey through parts of his realm. Some commentators suggest that this is a desire for them to be alone, but 8:4 indicates that the daughters of Jerusalem have travelled with them. Therefore while she longs to discover her Beloved's possessions, she also wants her fellow disciples to be with her as he points out the features of his kingdom to her.

What is remarkable in this desire is that she is taking the lead, as it were, by asking him to come with her. She is not being presumptuous in making this suggestion. Rather this is a picture of the spiritual boldness that a restored backslider can exhibit in prayer. And it is clear that the Beloved was delighted to honour her request.

When we pray, we should ask Jesus to take us on a journey through his domains. In this life we can only ask him to take us through the kingdom of grace, but in the next life we will be taken by him on journeys throughout the kingdom of glory. Although the kingdom of glory contains many sites not found in the kingdom of grace, there are in the latter many wonderful places to visit.

Her words point to the varied nature of fellowship with Jesus. She mentions four different places: fields, villages, vineyards, a house (doors in v. 13 point to a building, perhaps a summer house). The field is a place of labour, the village is a place of rest, the vineyards are a place of examination, and the house is a place of sharing.

In the fields

The first location of fellowship with Jesus is the fields. In the fields, the servants of the King would be employed. Within Christ's kingdom there are many fields in which his people can exercise their gifts by working for him. There is the field where his people gather to pray, there is the field where the gospel is declared, there is the field where acts of kindness are done in his name.

The disciple may want to observe these fields because they give her great joy as she sees her Beloved's kingdom expanding in different ways. And when he is with her she also senses his joy at its growth. Or she may have gone to see the fields in order to have information about which she could speak to him. She may wonder why there is great activity in one field and little activity in another. The best person to consult regarding these matters is Jesus himself. This would be a picture of a believer interceding for the various situations within Christ's kingdom. Or she may have gone to the fields in order to work in them herself. When she goes into a field in this state of soul, she will be greatly helped because Jesus is with her. When she enters the field of prayer, she senses the presence of Christ. In the field of good deeds, she is aware of the help of Jesus. And she can work in other fields at the same time as she is in the field of prayer.

In the villages
The villages are the places where those who served the king lived. This is where their homes were located to which they returned after their day's work in order to rest and recuperate so to have strength to perform further work for their king. The villages are pictures of the locations where Christ's disciples obtain rest. Just as she wanted Jesus with her when she went to the fields, she knows that she needs to have Jesus with her in order to obtain rest. I don't think it is difficult to imagine the villages as a picture of the means of grace, the places where rest is given to weary souls – weary not only because of sin and temptation but also because of the energy they put forth in serving Christ.

Work for Jesus must be done in his strength and be followed by his means of recovery. Just as he said to the disciples when they returned from a mission in which they had been working for him, so Jesus says to us after we have done some work for him, 'Come away by yourselves to a desolate place and rest a while' (Mark 6:31). We can see that workers would often come home with minor injuries and bruises that needed nursing; they would be hungry and longing for food; they would need a comfortable place to rest. From a spiritual perspective, it is sweet to take Jesus with us as we finish our toil and enjoy receiving him as the tender physician, the plentiful and satisfying food for our souls, and the comfortable place of rest.

In the vineyards

The third place of fellowship is the vineyards where she wants his help in assessing the progress of the vines and other fruits. This is probably a reference to the practice of self-examination. It is worth noting that this desire for ongoing assessment comes from a spiritually-healthy believer. There are at least two possible reasons for this.

First, believers can have assurance and not fully realise the spiritual state of their souls. 'Although believers be clear as to their interest (as the Bride was, v. 10), yet may they be indistinct as to the knowledge of their own condition, and therefore ought not to neglect this duty of self-examination: but where the clearness is solid, they will be the more careful in the searching of themselves.'[1] It is often the case that believers fall after they have had a mountain-top experience, when they did not anticipate the relapse. Even when enjoying the Saviour's presence and provision, they should be praying, 'Search me, O Lord.'

Second, her recollection of past experiences would lead her to be careful. After all, she had known times of assurance in the past and yet she had succumbed to spiritual laziness. Having been restored, she did not want to repeat her past mistakes; therefore she wanted Jesus to help her examine her progress in the life of grace. Self-examination should enable us to avoid the pitfalls of the past.

It is important to stress that she asks Jesus to help her in her self-examination. Sometimes believers are prone to take Moses (the law) with them when they engage in this duty. The law of God is good, and healthy believers desire to live up to its requirements. It is inevitable that a Christian will discover flaws and failings when she examines herself. If she has the law with her, all it will do is condemn her for her faults. It will not commend her progress because her development is not perfect. But Jesus will encourage her

---

1   James Durham (1840, 1997), p. 394.

imperfect progress and he will forgive her faults when she and he together find them. The gracious Saviour accepts and blesses imperfect acts of dedication from his disciple. He delights in her growth in grace, even though she is not perfect.

Another aspect of self-examination that is seen in her words is the reality that self-examination takes time. She wants to get 'early' to the vineyards. It was common for people in the Middle East to rise with the sun. Her words indicate that self-examination is not an activity that can be done in a short space of time; rather it is the equivalent of a full day's work. One reason for the necessity of ample time is her desire to examine everything in her vineyards. A healthy believer wants to scan her entire soul in order to assess her state and to increase her spiritual vitality.

The proper response to true self-examination is depicted in her resolve to show her love to the king in the vineyard once they have examined the state of the fruits. Similarly, a believer, having gone through the experience of having Jesus help her in the duty of self-examination, finds plenty reasons for expressing her love for him. She discovers afresh that despite her sinfulness she is accepted in him; that despite her failure to grow as she should have done, he is pleased with what she does for him; that despite her period of backsliding she is welcome to know him more intimately, and to experience his grace more fully.

In the building
The fourth place of fellowship with Jesus takes place within a building (v. 13), which may have been a summer house in the vineyard or somewhere else. In this building, she had placed fragrant plants and pleasant fruits for the enjoyment of her Beloved. Some of these fruits are old, others are fresh. She had gathered them from the vineyard, not for her own benefit but for his enjoyment.

When we are enjoying Jesus' company, it is appropriate for us to tell him about what he did for us in the past as well as what he is enabling us to experience in the present. For example, we can bring forward our first exercise of faith in him, not because it was our activity, but because it appeared as a result of his work in our souls. Or we can mention answers that we have received to our prayers, not because of the genius of the prayers, but because of the gracious way they were answered.

At the same time it is necessary that we have fresh results of his grace on display in order to delight him. Faith is not only in the past, it is to be active in the present. Love should be marked by gratitude for recent blessings as well as previous ones. This combination of old and new brings great delight to the king. Of course, it is wonderful that he should so value our little contributions. But he does, and this awareness should remove fear from us, even if we are returning backsliders.

She   ¹Oh that you were like a brother to me
who nursed at my mother's breasts!
If I found you outside, I would kiss you,
and none would despise me.
²I would lead you and bring you
into the house of my mother –
she who used to teach me.
I would give you spiced wine to drink,
the juice of my pomegranate.
³His left hand is under my head,
and his right hand embraces me!
⁴I adjure you, O daughters of Jerusalem,
that you not stir up or awaken love until it pleases
(Song 8:1-4).

24

The Restored Disciple wants more Fellowship

Song of Solomon 8:1-4

Verses 1-4 are the second half of the woman's response to the king's expressed delight in her. In the previous verses (7:11-13), the king and the woman have been exploring his domains, looking at his fields and his villages; his fields are places of labour and the villages are where his servants live and receive refreshment and rest from him. Then they went to examine the vineyards to see if there were any thriving fruits; this was a picture of self-examination. The self-examination was followed by the woman giving to him old and new fruit to enjoy in a location made fragrant with the aroma of flowers. This activity depicts a recovered believer giving glory to Christ for all the spiritual developments that have occurred in her life. Having gone so far through this process, she now desires to spread wider her delight in him.

1. Desire for public display of love (v. 1)

It seems to be the case that in many parts of the Middle East it was, and is, inappropriate for a husband and wife to embrace in public. The persons that would embrace in public would be brothers and sisters. They would have grown up together and there would be no hint of anything improper when they embraced. The disciple in the poem uses this social custom to express what she now wants to demonstrate to her Beloved. The disciple wants to kiss the king in the presence of others. Until now, as she went to the fields and the villages she had been in his company, but those who observed them would not have noticed how strong her feelings were for him. Spiritually speaking, what kind of kisses can a disciple give to Jesus in public?

First, there is the kiss of *reconciliation*, which would show that she is now at peace with him. This type of kiss can be used in an evangelistic sense when we tell others that we have found the Saviour, that he has forgiven us our sins, and brought us into an eternal union with him. Second, there is the kiss of *gratitude*, which would show how thankful she was for the deliverance that she had experienced. She had a double reason for thankfulness: the king had not only brought her into a personal union with himself, he had also restored her when later she had failed to respond to his expressions of love. Third, there is the kiss of *adoration*, which would show that her experience of his grace had enabled her to see how great a king he is. His actions in forgiving her and restoring her had given her windows into his great heart of love. It is similar with us; each contact with Jesus should increase our perception of his immense glory. With increasing fervency of worship, we should say to him, 'Who is a God like you, pardoning iniquity and passing over transgression for the remnant of his inheritance? He does not retain his anger forever, because he delights in steadfast love' (Micah 7:18).

If a devoted wife would have behaved like this in everyday life, she would have caused shame to her husband and herself. This disciple had not been devoted to Christ, yet in the poem, she affirms that should she embrace Christ in a public way, she would not be despised by him. The Saviour is not embarrassed by public displays of love from failed disciples. The reality is the opposite – he is delighted when we spontaneously show the world that we want to kiss him. The writer to the Hebrews reminds us that Jesus is not ashamed to call his people his brethren (Heb. 2:11).

2. Desire for a private display of love (vv. 2-3)

The woman also wanted to take the king to a special place, to her mother's house. Her words here are similar to what she says in 3:4-5, which detail her response on a previous occasion when she was restored from the experience of having lost a sense of fellowship with the king. On that occasion, she wanted to take the king to her home, where she lived. It is a picture of personal fellowship with Jesus.

Personal devotion is the place of *instruction* for a disciple. There is a question about how to translate the clause rendered 'she who used to teach me'. Older translations and commentators regarded it as meaning, 'there you shall teach me,' that is, the king would give personal instruction to a devoted disciple as she takes him to this special location. The obvious example that comes to mind is Mary who chose to sit at the feet of Jesus and received personal instruction from him. A heart full of love is the heart that will understand most about what Jesus has to say.

Personal devotion is the place of *sharing* by a disciple. In this place of delightful intimacy, there is a response from the disciple. In the poem she gives him a drink of spiced pomegranate wine. It was common for people to add spices to such drinks in order to enhance the taste. The woman has taken some fruit and, by adding spices to it, she has made a drink suitable for the king to enjoy. Both the pomegranate and the spices come from her vineyard (her heart). Some of the spices are bitter and others are sweet. This drink is made up of her development in the life of grace and of appropriate feelings that mark her growth. She has the bitterness of repentance and the sweetness of love to give to her Master.

Personal devotion is the place of *satisfaction* for Christ. His contentment is seen in his posture of resting. This is the second time that Jesus and his disciple have been portrayed in this way (see 2:6). The difference between that previous occasion and this latter one is that she is now a restored backslider whereas previously she had been an earnest seeker. Yet she is in the place of enjoying the Saviour's affections. In Isaiah 66:1, God asks, 'Where is the place of my rest?'(KJV). The next verse gives the answer: 'But this is the one to whom I will look: he who is humble and contrite in spirit and trembles at my word.' Zephaniah 3:17 says: 'The LORD your God is in your midst, a mighty one who will save; he will rejoice over you with gladness; he will quiet you by his love; he will exult over you with loud singing.'

Personal communion is also the place of *strength*. The king is depicted here as holding up her head. We need divine strength for many reasons. It is required in order to enjoy the love of Jesus (Eph. 3:16-19). This strength is also given to enable disciples to continue in the Christian life: 'He gives power to the faint, and to him who has no might he increases strength. Even youths shall faint and be weary, and young men shall fall exhausted; but they who wait for the LORD shall renew their strength; they shall mount up with wings like eagles; they shall run and not be weary; they shall walk and not faint' (Isa. 40:29-31). God is our refuge and strength (Ps. 46:1). Yet, as Paul discovered, this strength is known along with our weakness (2 Cor. 12:9).

Fifthly, personal communion is the place of *solace*, where Jesus comforts his disciple. Here the hand of the king is embracing her. It is a picture of great tenderness and gentleness. Jesus draws near and sweetly assures his disciple of his great love to her. He will remind her of his great and precious promises that detail his interest in her and his intention to do great things for her.

3. Admonition not to disturb love (v. 4)

The woman turns to the daughters of Jerusalem who are aware of the great delight she and the king are having in each other. She turns to them because she does not want them to disturb his rest. I suspect she does not want them to distract her from focussing on her Beloved. This is another reminder that sometimes a disciple's fellowship with Jesus can be interrupted by fellow Christians speaking about inappropriate matters. Such matters need not be worldly, merely unsuitable to say to a person who is enjoying the love of Jesus. They could include speaking about religious matters as well as secular ones. We need to be sensitive to one another in case we disrupt spiritual intimacy.

This long poem within the Song, which had begun with the woman refusing to let the king into her location (5:2), closes with the woman now enjoying the presence of the king. Her experience had taught her the importance of maintaining a spiritually-healthy relationship with the Lover of her soul and she did not want it to be affected adversely, even by her friends.

Poem 8

After the Mountain Top (8:5-14)

Daughters: ⁵Who is that coming up from the wilderness, leaning on her beloved?

The King: Under the apple tree I awakened you. There your mother was in labour with you; there she who bore you was in labour.

She: ⁶Set me as a seal upon your heart,
as a seal upon your arm,
for love is strong as death,
jealousy is fierce as the grave.
Its flashes are flashes of fire,
the very flame of the Lord.
⁷Many waters cannot quench love,
neither can floods drown it.
If a man offered for love
all the wealth of his house,
he would be utterly despised (Song 8:5-7).

25

Parting can be sweet

Song of Solomon 8:5-7

A new poem within the Song begins with verse 5. The speaker is observing the arrival of the king and the one he loves. Often this verse is interpreted as describing the Christian life. The wilderness is the world and the Christian is leaning on Jesus as he takes her through it. But we know that there are times when our relationship to Jesus cannot be described as leaning on his breast.

Instead of describing an ongoing state of affairs in the Christian life that is going to continue until Jesus and the believer reach heaven, I think the verse is picturing the close of a journey the king and the woman have made together. It may be that they are returning from the journeys described in the closing verses of the previous poem. Verse 14 will indicate that the king has left after bringing her to this location, so their destination here could not have been heaven. Instead the king has brought her to a suitable place where he could leave her with her companions.

A difficulty arises when we think of the term 'wilderness'. Usually we imagine a barren area without growth or life. It is better to think of it as uncultivated land as opposed to cultivated areas. It could be a place of danger from wild animals or from robbers, where a traveller would need provision as he passed through. Nevertheless it was part of Solomon's country, and not part of the territory of his enemy. Solomon was able to travel through it freely, no doubt in a carriage guarded by soldiers. Out in these wild areas he may have had lodging houses where he could meet with his friends.

When we think of Jesus, we recall that he is Lord of all. Both the cultivated fields and the wild areas of the world are his. The cultivated places are where his grace has produced spiritual vitality, where the laws of his kingdom are gladly obeyed – these places would be the congregations of his people. Yet his followers are not able to spend all their time in these cultivated areas. Daily they have to go through wild areas, and in these areas they need provision, protection from danger and assurance of safety. The only way that these can be received is for Jesus to accompany each of them as they pass through these wild areas. This is being pictured here. Jesus and his disciple have been travelling together and are returning to her abode, where her companions are looking out for her. As they observe them drawing near, they are focussed, not on the king, but on the nearness that the disciple enjoys to him. They observe that this journey to the wild places has increased her devotion to the king and opened up for her increased opportunities of intimacy with him. When a disciple of Jesus experiences his provision in a spiritually-barren place and observes his protection in a spiritually-dangerous place, her devotion should increase.

Her posture is a wonderful picture of healthy faith. It depicts delight in his company, an example of Calvin's comment that 'faith is the warm embrace of love'. But it also depicts dependence upon him because she is leaning upon him, aware of both her weakness and his strength.

The king details his love (5b)
There has been disagreement about who is speaking in verse 5b about the fruit tree. The pointing of the Massoretic text indicates that it is the woman (Durham, for example, takes this view). Yet the majority of Christian fathers and other commentators refer it to the king. The way to decide who is speaking is to assess which speaker the words fit best.

If it is the woman who is speaking, then she says that she woke him from sleep while they were passing a particular fruit tree, which was the place where the king had been born. Perhaps the tree was planted to celebrate that fact or else his mother suddenly went into labour there and gave birth. In any case, the woman focuses on a particular event in his life. On a spiritual level, such activity is very appropriate for the disciples of Jesus. In his company they should speak of events in his life, so displaying to him their love for him.

If it is the king that is speaking, then he is claiming to have been involved in her birth and upbringing. Obviously he does not mean that he is her father. Literally, the verse does not make sense if applied to Solomon and a lover, but it does make sense if applied spiritually to Christ because he was instrumental in giving new life to each of his disciples. Earlier in the Song the king was likened to a fruit tree (2:3). Literally, Solomon could not be the tree under which his lover was born. But sinners are born again and grow in grace through receiving from the fruits that Jesus delights to give freely to them. He is the tree that provides shade from the heat of God's wrath, fragrance to dispel the stench of their sin, and fruit to feed their souls.

Therefore I would suggest that this poem describes the daughters of Jerusalem overhearing what the king and the disciple are saying to one another. In verse 5b, he speaks to the disciple about her birth and in verses 6 and 7 she responds.

Desiring his love (v. 6)

Although she has been enjoying his intimacy, the woman's words reveal that she was anticipating his absence. When she says, 'Set me as a seal upon your heart, as a seal upon your arm,' she is using the words that a wife would say to her husband if he was going to be away from their home. She would want him to so impress her image on his heart so that he would not forget her. The disciple, sensing they are drawing near to her house, addresses Jesus and requests that she be engraved on his heart.

This is not the first time that she has been in a house without his presence. In 2:8-13, the king is pictured as coming there in order to enjoy her company for a short time before he goes away again (2:14-17). It was probably to her house that he had come on that occasion when she had denied him access (5:2ff), a response that had resulted in deep searchings of heart before they were once again together. Now that she is going to her house again, she wants from him the assurance that, when he is absent, he will be thinking about her.

The Christian life can be described in many ways. It is a race, a fight, an ascent; it is also a romance in which the Beloved comes and visits the one he loves. They love each other, yet there are times when he expresses his love in strength to her heart. Such occasions are mountain-top experiences, but they don't last all the time. And we are not to expect them all the time. Instead we are to remind ourselves that they occur for our spiritual benefit, and like all other such benefits we should pray that they would be blessed to us.

Moody Stuart comments on this verse, 'Ransomed one, in the hour of thine access lift not thy head from that bosom, till thou hast pleaded and procured the engraving of thy name upon that heart.' It is not sufficient to plead for this reality, we have also to pray until we have procured it. He further comments: 'The fruit of many interviews with Jesus is partially lost for want of this wisdom and zeal; lost by not covenanting with him before the meeting is dissolved, that there shall be this perpetual remembrance; lost by not detaining him till he grant this perpetual remembrance.' [1] We are to be like Jacob when he responded to a divine visit by saying to the Lord, 'I will not let you go unless you bless me' (Gen. 32:26).

We can picture a wife saying to her husband as he is about to leave for a long journey, 'Tell me that you will think about me when you are away!' The plea does not arise from doubt, but from her need of comfort. Jesus knows that we will need comfort, but we have to ask him for it.

Describing her love (vv. 6-7)

The woman describes her love as determined, jealous, intense, indestructible and beyond value. It is as determined as death (it will follow him at all costs), it is jealous for anything that might come between herself and her Beloved, it is more intense than a raging fire, it is indestructible (a great storm cannot destroy it), and it is of more value than what a person possesses. These features should be true of marital love, and they are seen in the heart of a believer towards her Master. Of course, her love for Jesus, although it contains these beautiful features, is only a faint expression compared to the love that he has shown, is showing, and will yet show to her. So what is his love like?

His love was determined in that no obstacle could prevent him becoming her husband. There was the obstacle of nature (he is divine, she is human, but he overcame it by becoming a man); there is the obstacle of sin (he is perfect, she was sinful, but he overcame it by his sacrifice on the cross and his giving of the Spirit); there

---

1 Alexander Moody Stuart (1857), p. 575.

will be the obstacle of death, but he will overcome it by the resurrection of his people.

His love was jealous as he observed her chasing other lovers. Today, jealousy is not regarded as a virtue because it is equated with envy. Yet jealousy is an aspect of God's character: 'You shall not bow down to them or serve them; for I the Lord your God am a jealous God, visiting the iniquity of the fathers on the children to the third and fourth generation of those who hate me, but showing steadfast love to thousands of those who love me and keep my commandments' (Deut. 5:9-10). Believers were the objects of Jesus' love before they were converted because they had been given to him by the Father. And he deposed the alternatives that they sought instead of him.

Further, his love for each of them is very intense. His desire for each of them is never weak, even when they are backsliding. The love of Jesus to them does not fluctuate according to their behaviour, although wrong behaviour can prevent him expressing that love in their hearts. When we backslide, the heart of Jesus yearns for our return. He longs with great desire for the time when all of his people will be with him for ever.

His love could not be destroyed by a great storm. There never was such a storm as Calvary when the deep waters of God's wrath against our sins descended in full force on the submerged Saviour. He lost a sense of God's love to him in the storm, but he never lost his awareness of his love for God nor did his love for his people decrease even a fraction as he endured their punishment.

And his love for us caused him to prize us above his possessions. He gave up the glory of heaven in order to set us free from sin. Although he was rich, for our sakes he became poor.

Of course, our love is not only an imitation of the love of Christ; it is also obtained by spending time with Christ.

The king and the disciple have been together, and as his visit comes to an end, she displays the benefit of having been in his company. The Spirit of love in Jesus was also in her, and that Spirit would remain with her through less profound and less intimate experiences.

Daughters: ⁸We have a little sister,
and she has no breasts.
What shall we do for our sister
on the day when she is spoken for?
⁹If she is a wall,
we will build on her a battlement of silver,
but if she is a door,
we will enclose her with boards of cedar.

She: ¹⁰I was a wall,
and my breasts were like towers;
then I was in his eyes
as one who finds peace.
¹¹Solomon had a vineyard at Baal-hamon;
he let out the vineyard to keepers;
each one was to bring for its fruit a thousand
  pieces of silver.
¹²My vineyard, my very own, is before me;
you, O Solomon, may have the thousand,
and the keepers of the fruit two hundred.

The king: ¹³O you who dwell in the gardens,
with companions listening for your voice;
let me hear it.

She: ¹⁴Make haste, my beloved,
and be like a gazelle
or a young stag
on the mountains of spices (Song 8:8-14).

26

Commitment

SONG OF SOLOMON 8:8-14

In the poem the king and his beloved have now arrived at the location where he is going to leave her. The daughters of Jerusalem had been looking out of the house as the king and his love were drawing near, and the daughters had heard the closing words of the couple's conversation. In verses 8 and 9 the daughters speak to both the king and the woman and she begins her reply in verse 10.

The dedication of the daughters (vv. 8-9)
The concern of the daughters is for their younger sister, to help make her ready for future meetings with the king. I would suggest that the little sister depicts a convert who has been a believer for a shorter period than the ones depicted by the daughters. The daughters, who speak as maturer believers, are concerned about her spiritual development. They proceed to say what their intention is, under the imagery of either a wall or a door. Probably they have in mind a wall that would go round a city or a door that gives entrance to a large building. These walls and doors could be unattractive to look at, and it was common to build palaces or turrets on the walls or to use beautiful wood to make the doors in order that the walls and the buildings would be pleasing to the eye. The

illustrations show how the daughters would help her develop into a mature believer. A turret would not be built overnight, it would take time. In addition to the commitment, there is also the suggestion of costly sacrifice (purchasing silver for the palaces or cedar for the doors). Prolonged commitment that is genuine is accompanied by cost and such should mark the involvement of more mature believers in the lives of younger believers. Often, there is an element of concern when we don't see sufficient signs of growth. Yet concern is not enough; in addition there has to be involvement in order to bring about the change.

The daughters had in mind what their little sister would look like when her marriage day came. Perhaps she had been promised to Solomon. Whether she had or not, it was love for her that caused them to want her to look her best when that day arrived. Similarly, believers should have in mind what other believers will look like on their marriage day, when they and the Saviour sit down at the marriage supper of the Lamb.

The devotion of the disciple (vv. 10-12)

The woman responds in verse 10. She takes one of the daughter's images (the wall) and applies it to herself. Towers have appeared on her wall, the evidence of development. She is aware of this change in her, but she knew something else as well – she had brought delight to her Beloved and had experienced his favour as a result. Her words are not merely a description of her progress; they are also an encouragement to the daughters concerning what can be achieved by mutual involvement in another believer's life.

The woman then proceeds to describe her dedication to the king. She alludes to Solomon's agreement with some tenants who leased a vineyard from him. It is likely that the vineyard had a thousand vines, with a shekel being paid for each. She then describes herself as a vineyard that should be dedicated to her Beloved. As she thinks of what he has done for her she desires to give everything she has to him.

We have here a picture of how a disciple should respond to her Master as they come to the end of a period of sweet fellowship together. She has been with Jesus enjoying his company and now he has brought her back to the house where her fellow disciples live. Coming back with him, she resolves to (a) be an encouragement to her fellow believers and (b) to dedicate herself to her Lord. This is how we should respond to Jesus after we have been to a conference or a communion, or after a private time when he revealed himself to our souls.

Spurgeon observed that the woman does not focus on other vineyards. 'The next time you are tempted to complain of some brother or sister, check yourself, and say, "It is my vineyard which is before me; there are some ugly thistles in it, and some great nettles over there in the corner. I have not trimmed my vines this summer; I have not taken the little foxes, which spoil the vines; but, henceforth, I will attend more diligently to 'my vineyard, which is mine'." A blessed way of keeping from finding fault with other people is to look well to your own vineyard.'[1]

The departure of the king (v. 13)

The king is about to leave, so he says to the woman, 'O you who dwell in the gardens, with companions listening for your voice; let me hear it.' With great delight he has listened to the conversation between the woman and the daughters. It is like the situation described in Malachi 3:16: 'Then those who feared the Lord spoke with one another. The Lord paid attention and heard them, and a book of remembrance was written before him of those who feared the Lord and esteemed his name.'

---

[1] C. H. Spurgeon (1860), A sermon entitled, 'Christ's Love for his Vineyard,' preached on a Thursday evening in the summer of 1860 and published for reading on June 29th, 1902.

But he is not only delighted in hearing their conversation with one another. He also wants to hear her speaking to him. One of the dangers that can occur after a time of rich experience of Jesus is that we can become so absorbed in describing to others what took place, that we forget to speak to him. Jesus wants to hear our voice. We can speak to him secretly, one to one; we can speak to him simultaneously, when we are speaking also to his disciples; we can speak to him sorrowfully, when we have sinned against him; we can speak to him submissively, when he has denied us our desires; we can speak to him lovingly, as we thank him for his mercy.

And we can note where he wants her to speak to him; he wants to hear her voice in the gardens. The gardens speak of cultivated places, where rest and refreshment can be found. They are a picture of the visible church with all its means of grace. Through these, the believer obtains everyday experiences from the Lord while he withdraws away from extraordinary encounters. In the gardens, they obtain the strength to continue serving the Lord.

Jesus wants to hear her voice in each part of the gardens. He desires to hear us in all the means of grace: at the prayer meeting, at the Sunday services, at the Lord's Supper, at other times of fellowship. The Saviour never tires of hearing what each of his people has to say to him.

The desire of the disciple (v. 14)
Having heard the king's parting exhortation, the disciple now utters the longing of her heart. Yes, she will remain in the gardens, enjoying his provision, but she will also be longing for him to return for another special encounter. She likens him to a speedy deer, able to cross rapidly the mountains that are between her and him: 'Make haste, my beloved, and be like a gazelle or a young stag on the mountains of spices.' In what ways can King Jesus appear?

Jesus will come *suddenly* to our souls. The imagery of the leaping deer suggests this. He may come in a special way at the next conference we attend or the next communion we enjoy; he may come as we are reading the Bible by ourselves or are speaking to him in prayer.

He will come *sweetly* when he draws near. These barriers will become mountains of spices because in order to cross them he will come from the mountain of myrrh (4:6), heaven. Whatever these mountains are, they become mountains of spices because the feet of Jesus run across them and the fragrances of the heavenly world perfume the atmosphere. Mountains that seemed dangerous will become sweet. As we look at these mountains from the gardens, we can be apprehensive. For example, ahead of us is the mountain of death, and what a dreadful fear it can cause. But when Jesus comes across this mountain, when its frightful appearance is made fragrant by his coming, then it will not be a source of terror. Or Jesus will come to deliver us when we feel that all is lost, when the breath of the devil is in our face, as we fear the worst, when providence seems against us, when we imagine that we are about to be overcome by danger. Then Jesus appears, and all is calm, just as it was for his disciples in the boat in the midst of the storm when he came to them walking on the sea.

He will come *finally* at the end of the age. What a wonderful visit that will be! It will be the time when this prayer will cease to be offered because from then on all believers will be forever with the Lord. When he comes in this most spectacular manner, we will see his great delight as by his almighty power he raises his people from the dead and transforms them, as well as those still alive, into his likeness. We will see him create the new heavens and the new earth and we will hear him say to us, 'Come and share my inheritance.'

Matthew Henry, in commenting on Song of Solomon 8:14, wrote: 'It is good to conclude our devotions with a joyful expectation of the glory to be revealed, and holy humble breathings towards it. We should not part but with the prospect of meeting again. It is good to conclude every sabbath with thoughts of the everlasting sabbath, which shall have no night at the end of it, nor any week-day to come after it. It is good to conclude every sacrament with thoughts of the everlasting feast, when we shall sit down with Christ at his table in his kingdom, to rise no more, and drink of the wine new there, and to break up every religious assembly in hopes of the general assembly of the church of the first-born, when time and days shall be no more: Let the blessed Jesus hasten that blessed day. Why are his chariot-wheels so long a coming? Why tarry the wheels of his chariots?'

It is precious to Jesus to recall that the closure of his time of special nearness with a disciple was marked by an affirmation of her love. She addresses him as 'my beloved'. He, too, longs for his second coming. But until then, may we have special visits from him, and may we entreat him lovingly to repeat them as often as he sees fit.

Bibliography

George Burrows (rpt. 1958), *Commentary on the Song of Solomon*, Banner of Truth.

James Durham (1840, rpt. 1997), *The Song of Solomon*, Banner of Truth.

E. W. Hengstenberg (1860), 'Prolegomena to the Song of Solomon' in *Commentary on Ecclesiastes and Other Treatises*, Smith, English and Co.

Alexander Moody Stuart (1857), *The Song of Songs*, James Nisbet.

Marcus Rainsford [n.d.], *The Song of Solomon*, Simpkin, Marshall, Hamilton and Kent.

Richard A. Norris (2003), 'The Song of Songs,' *The Church's Bible*, Eerdmans (very useful for comments by various church fathers and medieval writers).

C. H. Spurgeon (1996), *The Most Holy Place*, Christian Focus.

J. Hudson Taylor (1914, rpt, 1996), *Union and Communion*, Christian Focus.

"...something beautifully positive and full of life for the congregation of believers, as well as seekers."
DOUGLAS KELLY

THE LORD'S SUPPER

MALCOLM MACLEAN

ISBN 978-1-84550-428-1

The Lord's Supper

Malcolm Maclean

A careful examination of the means and practice of the Lord's supper. Malcolm Maclean seeks to encourage us to focus on the Lord Jesus who is the head as we celebrate the Lord's supper.

Malcolm Maclean's study of the biblical basis, historical development and practical administration of the Lord's Supper in our churches is a rich blend of scholarly analysis and pastoral insight. The question of what Jesus is doing in the Lord's Supper rather than what we are doing challenges the subjectivism that drives much of our practice, and restores a much needed emphasis on the Supper as a means of grace. This study is highly recommended.

Iain D. Campbell,
Minister, Point Free Church of Scotland, Isle of Lewis

...something beautifully positive and full of life for the congregation of believers, as well as seekers.

Douglas F. Kelly,
Richard Jordan Professor of Theology,
Reformed Theological Seminary, Charlotte, North Carolina

A veritable tour de force ...which will be of interest to the entire church. Maclean's handling of the subject is comprehensive and sure-footed, delving into practical areas of frequency and observance as much as the theological principles that underpin the Communion Service. A timely and important book that will aid in the rediscovery of importance and function of the sacrament of the Lord's Supper in the life of the church.

Derek Thomas,
Minister of Preaching and Teaching,
First Presbyterian Church, Columbia, South Carolina

Christian Focus Publications
publishes books for all ages

Our mission statement –

STAYING FAITHFUL
In dependence upon God we seek to impact the world through literature faithful to His infallible Word, the Bible. Our aim is to ensure that the Lord Jesus Christ is presented as the only hope to obtain forgiveness of sin, live a useful life and look forward to heaven with Him.

REACHING OUT
Christ's last command requires us to reach out to our world with His gospel. We seek to help fulfil that by publishing books that point people towards Jesus and help them develop a Christ-like maturity. We aim to equip all levels of readers for life, work, ministry and mission.

Books in our adult range are published in three imprints:

Christian Focus contains popular works including biographies, commentaries, basic doctrine and Christian living. Our children's books are also published in this imprint.

Mentor focuses on books written at a level suitable for Bible College and seminary students, pastors, and other serious readers. The imprint includes commentaries, doctrinal studies, examination of current issues and church history.

Christian Heritage contains classic writings from the past.

Christian Focus Publications Ltd,
Geanies House, Fearn, Ross-shire,
IV20 1TW, Scotland, United Kingdom.
www.christianfocus.com